THE ORGIA KHRONICLES

John 'Karneios' Auletta

Dionysus

THE ORGIA KHRONICLES

Copyright 2020 John 'Karneios' Auletta

No part of this book may be used or reproduced in any manner whatsoever without written permission from the publisher except in the cast of brief quotations and articles of review.

Table of Content

Dedication vii

Acknowledgements viii

Words From The Author..xii

Introduction 1

The Mask 4

Nascent (Quotes, Adages & Dramatic Word Play) 5

Poetic Inspiration (Raging Iambics)......................... 118

Thriambos Offerings (Triumphal Hymns)............................ 166

The Charge Of Dionysus 189

Epithets Of Dionysus (His Many Masks) 193

Known Facts About Dionysus (Just To Name A Few)....... 196

A Dionysian Afterthought (My Underworld Journey)......... 199

About The Author John Phillip Auletta (1985 -), ... 205

Dedication

This complex Journal is for You, My Beloved Dionysus. Lover of the Dance of Intoxicated Madness, Father of exuberant life. This Journal symbolizes my Dionysian Diversity, the Diversity that mirrors Your very Nature. Its pages of Pleasurable Wisdom is an Offering to Your Ecstatic Love, Chaos and constant presence in my life.

May this written experience be blissful to Your eyes and ears.

May Your ways forever be within every Dance step I take...

I love You to Death and Life...

          Io Euoi Bios Dionusou

ACKNOWLEDGEMENTS

In putting this book together, I've drawn on the wisdom and experience of my Pagan lifestyle, Witchcraft, Street/Urban knowledge and my Dionysian nature. However, I do not speak for the whole of Paganism or Dionysianism, nor should I. But I do owe honor to the Pagan elders, Witch familiars, Hiereia (Dionysian Priestesses), Maenads, and Wiccan High Priestesses who gladly shared their priceless wisdom with me.

All Blessed Be Io Euoi Io Euoi Bios Dionusou...

My Ecstatic Heartfelt Thanks go to:

* All my ancient Maenads, Satyrs and Bacchants whose ways inspired me to bring their Ecstatic experiences back to life in my own unique way. Holy Mania!!!

* Thanks to all my wonderful Aurics (ATD) and Dionysian Pagans who embody this Ecstatic Path with me: Dakota 'Slip' White (my Satyr bro 4Life, never doubt the fact that Dionysus brought us together), Twist, Sir Quan (never forgot about you, bro), Lady Rebekka (Gypsy goddess), Gaea, Ally Cat, Sannion, Lacy Bryde,

Denise Major-Dodge, Picasso (The Black Buddha), Vikki Bramshaw, Samantha Frye, Sarah Kate Istra Winter, Syna, Renee Rhodes, Ariade, Dar Psyche Alexander, WhiteBoy Mark, Silly Witches Coven, Lord Mitch, Maenads.Paris, Jan Clifford, Terry 'Joker' Weatherbed and to all those who have a place in their heart for Dionysus. Oceanwitchboy!!!!

* Broadest Thanks to my gorgeous family who supported me during the writing of this book and for the time they took out to help shape its glory—esp my beautiful niece Aquillah Roberson. My lil goddess Liyah Baddy who keeps a smile on my face. You're the best and your beauty is goddesslike—let nobody tell you different. To my two sisters and mother. You're the reason my connection to the goddess is so solid. Y'all give me a true love that only a Goddess gives Her children.

* A special thanks goes to my Pagan elders: Anne Newkirk Niven, Ashleen O'Gaea and Lady Passion for taking out their time to reply to all my letters. Anne your magazines (Witches & Pagans and Sage women) has truly brought magick to my situation. Ashleen your book (Enchanted Encumbered) has given me new ways to experience the Lord and Lady. And Lady Passion, your criticism and advice is well appreciated. True Story!!! And to my beautiful goddess of Mercy... who embodies the beauty of the Dark... and to my Wonderful Editor Ann Attwood. Thank you for being so patient with me.

* An Ecstatic Blessing to All my Temple Of Dionysus Family Members: Brandie Elaine Ross, Kirby Clarke, Tamara Wyndham, Erdem Kutlu, Anslaigh Eanruig O Dalaigh, and to any other Dionysian I may have missed… Io Euoi Bios Dionusou

* I give a blissful Thanks to Molly Hill for being the best friend I never had. All the nights you stayed up with me in beautiful conversation. I truly appreciate how you never judged me and how you showered me with endless friendship. Lol And my beautiful bestie Katreena Curtis.. Our Spider Connection!!

* Don Honor to my DG Family for still believing in me. Big ups to EmK, Menace, Skooda B, Mr.DeeGee47, Fendi (my motherfuckin Don), and Skrilla. No Mercy to my MG'z, Horns up: Don Kush (Your loyalty is priceless), Ziggy Da Great (never doubted me for one second) Don Squirt (Always made it better for WE), Don Wolf (my day one), Don Uni (nigga, I love you boi, words can't explain what WE been through). Don Gunnz (solid to the Horn), Don Ghost (We all We got) and to every MG Don and Donna-No Mercy!!!

* Blood Love to all my Bros: Big 20 (I love you Phat Boi, East 2 West), Tik Tok (it's been over ten years and We still showing niggas how it's done, Don 2 Da Fruits), Solo Ru (you always understood me bro, thanks for that love), Big Pooh (I'll still hurt a nigga about you, word life), D5 (I'll never forget the Love you've shown me and still show, Don 2 Da Lanes), Rikko Billy (Don 2 Da 9s), A1 Shine, A1 Billy and Yano (I've watched you grow).

* And last, but not least, Thank you Great Dionysus for giving me a heart that is truly wild and free yet it's humble and it's me. I love you with Enraptured Love & Ecstatic Trust, as I gaze upon Your beast, You sharpen my Horned Sun which evokes the purest Lust.

Io Euoi Timai...

WORDS FROM THE AUTHOR

"What does my Dionysian journal say about me?" is a question I wrestled with for a while before I sat down to put this book together. During the process of writing it, I wanted this book to give people a sense of how I see and experienced Dionysus (My World) in the forms of quotes, prayers, jewels, metaphoric adages, unique questions and thoughts. However, words cannot express the true beauty of the Dionysian Mysteries, only experience can—the body knows His (Dionysus) truth. Dionysus' Mysteries to US (Those who walk the path *The Way Of The Satyr*), are like Love, Inner Visions, Insights—which are often simple ones. If they seem esoteric to the uninitiated (Not of The Way Of The Satyr), it is not out of deception or intention to hide (secrecy), but because words are powerless to account for them. That's the secrecy that defines OUR Mysteries... yet the Masked diverse forms of wisdom I use within this book, be it in quote or jewel form, are soaked in experience, humor, pleasure, magick and love. They are expressions of my Dionysian personality and spirituality.

In fact, wisdom and humor are closely related. The word "witan", meaning "wit", from which we get words like "wisecrack" and "wiseacre" are associated with wisdom. So, with that said, please have a sense of humor when you come across me being a wisecrack, or should I say "wiseass". Also, humor played a huge part in Priapos (Dionysus' son) worship. Now perhaps a quote or jewel isn't for you directly, however it could be for someone else. Dionysian wisdom is not dogmatic, so therefore I give you my experiences and wisdom in quotes, prayers, jewels, etc... but I am not teaching you of the Mysteries. You are taking from it what you may and transforming these words of wisdom to suit your own pursuits. I want you to see this book as a colorless Mask of wisdom, and you may add whatever color you like to this Mask so that it helps you inspire your own wisdom. In so many ways, my Dionysian journal is a biography in thought forms or quote forms. The books we write tell our stories for us, sometimes in ways we cannot imagine. It truly feels like in sharing my poetry, quotes and jewels, I share my Love deeper, because I'm giving you something deeper than words...

Now come experience Dionysus through the Masked eyes of my essence—which I call My Dramatic Arts.

                Ecstatically Yours,
        Sir John Auletta (Karneios Theones)

"Laughter has the power to banish sorrow and other ills, connecting it to Priapos' many apotropaic functions".

        (Masks Of Dionysus)
        -H. Jeremiah Lewis

Introduction

I chant that these words are used as instruments (flutes) of wisdom, so that what I write is of the soundest pleasure and will serve the beautiful side of truth. First and foremost I know many will wonder why such an ecstatic title for this book? I'm glad you have asked. The word 'Orgia' is the name of an ancient celebration of the Greek God Dionysus, and the very essence of Dionysus represents the way a person seeks ecstasy through direct experience or passion. Through experience with Him, He shows us how to have blessed enthusiasm for life. And by reading my quotes, poetry, and adages, you will begin to understand my direct experience with my passion for Dionysus. These quotes and adages are an ecstatic journey towards my blessed enthusiasm of Him.

FUN FACT: The word enthusiasm derives from the Greek word 'entheos' which means a god within or inspired by god. Of course Dionysus is within, however, I can't say that only one god inspired me to put my experiences and perceptions into forms of quotes and adages, yet I can say that many of the old Pagan gods played a part within my journey of life.

Now as for the word 'Resipiscent', it means to be made wise by experience. My goal is to share the wisdom I have gained by experience, in hopes that your experience as you read it is one that evokes your own power and wisdom. And remember, experience is not what happens to you, it is what you do with what happens to you. Nothing ever becomes real until it is experienced—even a motto is no motto to you until Dionysus (Life) has illustrated it. And that is the wisdom of The Way Of The Satyr...

An 'Adage' is a motto which is a brief sentence based on a long experience. Within every poem, quote and adage I have created, it will give you a brief glimpse into my inner world of a long experience with Dionysus in His many diverse forms. Now you understand why the title of my book is so ecstatic and personal. Dionysiac wisdom is a life that knows it is living.

In seeing the power of Dionysus within, one must realize that the whole of deity means *all* aspects of being, not just the good ones. So, within these poems, jewels, adages and thoughts, I'll express to you my multitude of Mask, including my street Mask (for Dionysus is the Mask), so keep in mind that every Mask I wear is my true face, but the Mask I wear will be the one that I feel is needed at that time. I am who I need to be when I need to be.

REMEMBER: Humans decay, cathedrals crumble, organizations fail, but Dionysiac wisdom and dramatic word-play endure. For every wise thought, there is another equally wise thought expressing precisely the opposite point of view. And with that said, allow my wise words to touch you within your own understanding. Empower yourself within your own way, for if something comes to life in others because of you, then you have made an approach to Mt. Nysa (immortality). And this is exactly how wisdom and dramatic word play endure. They live on through the people in their own way... However, a lot of my quotes may seem contradictory, that's because these quotes have been created throughout my journey. I am growing constantly, not the same as I once was. And as for the adages, I know it may seem all over the place, without a precise order, yet remember, order has no place within my Dionysian path, or with Dionysus.

So, welcome to the inner world of my being, I chant you emerge from it with something learned.

-All Blessed Be-

**Dionysian: adj. Wildly Pagan; Sensual. (The American Century Dictionary).

The Mask

My face is a Mask.
There is nothing beneath it.
Wear me and you will truly live.
Reject me and none will know your name.

I make miracles happen
through the fire and the vine and the Mask.

Put me on like a fine fawn skin
and know the truth that cannot be spoken
but is understood by all blessed initiates.

I, Dionysus ,have spoken these words of Wine.
Understand them and live forever,
the sweet fruit of the vine.

-H. Jeremiah Lewis

NASCENT

(Quotes, Adages & Dramatic Word Play)

** Dionysus has no Temple to house a guest in

But a Woodland forest bed for All to rest in

That the chaotic Satyrs and Mad Maenads nest in

He has no spiritual light hands to fold you

But the five-fingered poisonous Ivy to hold you

Out amongst Nysa where the ecstatic current rolled you.

1. I am nothing less than the holes upon a flute, stroked by the fingers of Pan... So that the whole world may hear Dionysus' melody.

(Inspired By: Anthesteria)

**Anthesteria is a great festival in honor of Dionysus, a time of enraptured joy and gloom. Celebrated with the newly-opened wine, uniting the dual aspects of The Mask. Listening to the beautiful Maenads playing the flute during the time of this great celebration inspired this quote. Anthesteria derives its name from the Greek word 'anthes' meaning "blossoming" or "flowering". In other words a festival for new beginnings, rebirth and vegetation.

2. Imagine all things horrible in its core essence, was an entity that sends US prayers for help & forgiveness. Can you imagine?

(Inspired By: Dionysian Madness)

**About sixteen years ago I was tripping on the magic mushrooms at a rave party and fell out. Friends said I was out for about three hours, during those three hours I had some very intense visions. I remember seeing a manifested force in the form of symbols, symbols that penetrated my heart with meaning, meaning that spoke of prayers. That vision inspired this quote.

3. Conquering or being conquered while fucking your lover is not an incentive, the exchange in itself is.

(Inspired By: My sexual experiences)

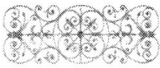

4. People are so damn futile that they will continue to stress themselves over the approval of others whom they have no love for.

(Inspired By: My Ego)

**In the summer of 2008, I attended a Pagan Festival in Boonville, NC, called the Pagan Wilderness Gathering. I met a Wiccan guy named... let's just say his name is Lord Savior. He asked me about the path I walked and I ended up telling him that Dionysus was my primary deity. He looked extremely shocked at me when I mentioned that to him, to which he replied, "How, when you're apparently not Greek?" Being that I was young at this time, his statement truly broke my heart, even though I knew my last name Auletta had Greek origins, which was connected to the Dionysian festivals. A man I'd never seen before broke my huge heart with one single statement, as if I sought his approval.

Years later I came to acknowledge, that yes, the Greek people of old preserved the tales of Dionysus, yet they belong to anyone who connects to them. The tales of my beautiful All Father Dionysus arose from many diverse landscapes, but the mysteries contained within them cannot be confined to one location(Greece). The mysteries they contain are Earth-Specific. They apply to everyone, anywhere, and any seeker who wishes to drink from the beautiful wine glass of madness and discover His secrets may do so. With that said, never stress over somebody's opinion or approval. Dionysus came to me in the form He felt was going to be the most relatable, for the gods draw substance from our imagination, even as They feed them. This may be what They want from us—to be inspired even as They inspire... and through that inspiration...They thrive.

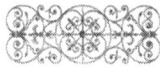

5. STREET JEWEL: Calculated intentions are far more dangerous than any man-made weapon. You wouldn't allow your adversary to have weapons, so why then should you allow them to have calculated intentions?

(Inspired By: The streets of Newark)

***Wisdom for All my DG Mercenaries... Horns up.*

6. Don't free women the burden of pain amongst their pregnancy or menstruation, because you may be freeing them the very essence of being a woman. Truthfully, giving birth and the menstrual cycle is very messy, painful, and often not the peak experience that women

seek to have. Yet however painful it is, women know it most definitely has its own meaning. A Dionysian Balance...

(Inspired By: The unique creation of Women)

**This is the pain I felt that the Maenads expressed during madness, pain with a purpose. Maenads are ecstatic female followers of Dionysus, His childhood Nurses and Companions.

7. Narrow minded Spirits cannot see universal truths.

(Inspired By: Conformist Christians)

**A Christian once told me that I'm narrow minded, because I see god in trees and shit. Of course, I laughed. I see Dionysus within All of Nature, including Trees. The beautiful thing about it is that in the days of old, one of Dionysus' aspects was called 'Endendros' (Tree).
So, who's actually narrow minded?

8. Never judge by labels, for deep within every stereotype there's always a very different unique truth.

(Inspired By: My Ex-Girl)

**She stereotyped me by saying I was super-freaked-out, because I worshipped the god of pleasure. There's some unique truth to this. Lol... It's a different truth that she might not understand though and that's why I believe she stereotyped me (labeled me).

9. This so called Devil is only powerful to those who created him in their own image and likeness.

(Inspired By: The Bible)

** Idols we adore are meaningful to us because we see ourselves in them.

10. I love embracing the Darkness because I get a kick out of enjoying and caressing Her ASSets. Lol.

(Inspired By: Dionysus Morychos (Dark One)

**When you learn to caress and enjoy the Dark soils, beautiful things come to bloom. Like one of Dionysus' other epithets, Anthios (god of all blossoming things).

11. Bravery is not the abandonment of fear, it is having the capacity to flow through it.

(Inspired By: Facing my own Daemons)

**I call my inner Daemon 'Agathos Daemon'... In the PGM IV 3165-3170, it mentions "O' holy Agathos Daemon, bring to fulfillment all favors and your divine oracles". Sometimes this world doesn't need an Angel, it needs a Daemon...

12. At times it is hard to separate which brooms I use to clear my path and the ones I use to dance. 'Aniconic'..

(Inspired By: The Brooms in my Broom closet)

**What does your broom mean to you? Or what tools do you use that help you both clear and celebrate your path? Tools that give balance are always the best to use. Remember that.

13. Your final moment is not as important as the moments that led up to it. By cherishing the journey, you come to respect the final destination.

(Inspired By: My Path's Journey)

**The Way Of The Satyr is my Dionysian Path. What comes at the end of that Path gets the same praise as the journey. As a Dionysian initiate, I celebrate in the harsh and the sterile no less than in the soothing and the fruitful. All aspects of life equally glorify ME, finding the ecstatic within every appearance.

14. Sometimes you have to have sex with Karma, just to see what She has under Her dress for you.

(Inspired By: My dance with Atropos(Fate)

**Atropos is the oldest of the Moirai (Fates), three goddesses of fate and destiny. Atropos is a daughter of Nyx, primordial goddess of the night. Atropos is the younger sister of the likes of Hemera, Aether, Hypnos, Oizys, Hesperides, and Oneiroi, and the older sister of the likes of Lachesis, Clotho, Apate and Eris.

Atropos was the oldest of the Three Fates, and was known as "the Inflexible One," or "inevitable." It was Atropos who chose the mechanism of death and ended the life of mortals by cutting their threads. She worked along with her two sisters, Clotho, who spun the thread, and Lachesis, who measured the length. Ampelos was a Satyr loved by the god Dionysus who was transformed by the Fates, or with the assent of the Fates, into a vine at death." (Ampelos, a youth loved by the god Dionysus, was killed by a bull.)

Dionysus, who never wept, lamented thus in his love, the awful threads of Moirai (Fate) were unloosened and turned back, and Atropos Neverturnback, whose word stands fast, uttered a voice divine to console Dionysus in sorrow, "He lives, I declare, Dionysus; your Satyr lives, and shall not pass the bitter water of Akheron (Acheron). Your lamentation has found out how to undo the inflexible threads of unturning Moirai (Fate), it has turned back the irrevocable. Ampelos is not dead, even if he died, for I will change your Satyr to a lovely drink, a delicious nectar. He shall be worshiped with the dancing beat of tripling fingers, when the double-sounding pipe shall strike up harmony over the feast, be it in Phrygian rhythm or Dorian tune, or on the boards a musical man shall sing him, pouring out the voice of Aonian reeds for Ismenians."

For Dionysus is so loved that even the Fates go against what's Fated... When I go I chant, Dionysus sheds those same tears so that the Fates make me immortal by His side.

15. If they say, "Sleep is the cousin of death," then I shall add that, "Celebration is the Horn child of life."

(Inspired By: Dionysus Karneios)

**Karneios is an epithet (aspect) of Dionysus which means The Horned Sun. Dionysus was born with Horns,* *not which connect Him to evil, but that connect Him to Nature, the wild side of Nature. Plus He was seen as the Nocturnal Sun. I adopted this title as my Pagan name due to many seeing me as the son of Dionysus along with the many people who said I act as if I have Horns on my head. However, I do see myself as the Horn Son(Sun) of Dionysus.*

16. In the midst of any war, be it political, religious, or the streets, you can become truly aware of what frightens your adversary most, by just paying close attention to the actions they use to scare you.

(Inspired By: Old street beef)

**During the summer of 2001 in the Bronx, NY, I was beefing with a guy over me Set (Gang) tripping on him. "Supposedly" he was a known guy in the hood. Things got out of hand and threats were made, but the actions he took against me failed. However, I used the same actions and realize this scared the shit out of him to the point he call for a peace treaty.*

17. Fear is only an issue if you allow it to paralyze you.

(Inspired By: Being chased by the Police)

18. Women are like flowers, pull a leaf and every layer reveals more hidden beauty.

(Inspired By: The Beauty of the Vulva)

***You ever aroused a female while watching her Pussy Lips slowly open up like a flower? It's a beautiful sight especially the scent...*

19. I see an incentive challenge in what others may see as broken.

(Inspired By: Life's Challenges)

***I was riding with one of my homies a while back. I'll never forget our conversation, because, for one, it was our last convo, and second, we were riding in my brand new 2003 BMW X5. We pulled up at my homie's project building. He saw one of his longtime friends from way back. She was looking really rough, and I can remember my homie showing out on her.*

When I pulled off, I asked him why he blew her off like that, and his reply was, "She's broken, bro. Nothing I can do with that."

I laughed at him and replied, "A woman's flaws and imperfections are what makes them beautiful and realistic."

20. My Dionysian adages act as continuing sources of poetic and dramatic inspiration, but because my adages are symbolic language of my experiences and always operate on more than one Masked level at a time, it is important to take into account the subliminal and pre-conscious levels at work as well as the conscious. For within my very adages, Dionysus awaits you.

(Inspired By: Dithyrambos)

**The Dithyrambos is a Dionysiac Hymn that embodies the very essence of Dionysus... He was the logos (the word) hundreds of years before Christ.

21. Sacred sex is like the poetry of the Universe, for it is both the rhyming rhythm of creation and chaos. And what I mean by chaos, is by getting lost in the exchange of pleasure with no sense of order, yet the flow still has rhythm and potential for creation.

(Inspired By: Dionysus)

**Summon Dionysus if you ever want to experience sacred sex with your lover. Here's an invocation I created to help summon Him. Light some Purple candles with Lavender incense, have a bowl of grapes to place all over your lover. It would be better to be upon a clearing in the woods, set up a date there with your lover. Then recite this:

'Invocation Of Dionysus'

I caress, I caress all earthly pleasures,
Amiss the chaotic essence of nature,
I seek upon your ecstatic madness,
I chant of desire, I chant of sadness,
Dancing with pain my blessed deliverance,
Enraptured in passion don't confuse me with
    innocence,
Call me within Darkness, in rage and anguish,
Summon me in wildness doesn't matter the language,
Invoke me in your honor
Experience my erotic energy,
Pleasure yourself with my beauty,
Keep to heart my lawless tendencies,
Drink with me on Nysa, a Mount of intense passion,
Within your own heart's deepest desire,
Grasp my Phallus in your hand
And bring forth my own divine fashion,
Purify yourself of guilt and shame,
Cum into my nature, release in my Name,
My Satyrs and Maenads are meant to be free,
Embodied with rapture and destruction-
    a mystic like me,
Frenzied, Pansexual and deeply unbound,
And surely not found by order's subtle sound,
No denial, No secretly pleasure untold,
Underworldly and Horned, Earthly and Bold,

        Io Euoi Io Euoi

22. In the process of writing poetry, treat it like a Christian, allow it to have blind faith in you. It must believe you're going to do right by it.

(Inspired By: A conversation with my poetry)

**I bet some of the best poets spoke to their poetry. What does your poetry say about you, literally?

23. I reject all answers that don't come from skin, soil, and bones. It is the Flesh of us and Earth that screams divinity.

(Inspired By: A Dionysian's connection to Earth)

**"My skin, my bones, my heretic heart are my authority.." Song by Catherine Madsen.

24. Absolutely nothing in this world exist which is not implicated in its own cause.

(Inspired By: The Bumble Bee)

**The Bumble Bee or Bees make up more than sixty-five percent of our food source due to their beautiful pollination. If you look closely at Nature with both your heart and eyes, you'll see that everything has their own

purpose. Fun Fact: Before Wine was sacred to Dionysus, He had Honey Mead (liquor) which made the Bee one of His sacred insects.

25. How do you battle an adversary who assumes the form of a memory?

(Inspired By: My Mental Health)

**Many have said "by burying it." Nope, tried that and it only made my adversary more powerful. Whenever we bury things within our subconscious, we give it life. Not just any life but supernatural life, because the subconscious is a very magickal place.

26. A heart full of gratitude is one that rarely misuses its gifts.

(Inspired By: The Wiccan Rede)

**"And it harm none, do as ye will."

27. It is much better to face Chaos with a Dionysian heart, so to appreciate wondrous pleasures—even though

at times they may be stained by pain—than to take status with the complaining souls, who neither rejoice in life nor suffered life, because they have lived in the dull realm that knows no pleasure or pain.

(Inspired By: Chaos Magick)

**Once you allow your heart to be the wild creature that it is, you'll start to notice how experiences become more beautiful. Our hearts are in cages (ribcage) for a reason. They're wild.*

28. The closest thing to god- is to experience the love of a nurturing mother.

(Inspired By: My Mother)

**I physically took my mother through the underworld and back and not one time has she ever stopped loving and nurturing me. She has the love that only a goddess can give.*

I love you ma, Always & Forever. Full Circle. Within those underworldly moments my mother also learned about herself, mirroring Dionysus' myth when He went to the underworld to save His mother.

29. Every Dionysian Pagan weaves their Thyrsus within their own essence and conjures up their own nature into existence.

(Inspired By: Ptolemy XII Auletes)

**My last name Auletta derives from Ptolemy Auletes. Auletes means a devoted flutist within the Dionysian festival and that's exactly what Ptolemy Auletes was, along with being a King. My Gramz said that he's my ancestor, even if it's just through the connection of our name. Ptolemy XII Auletes was also known as Neo Dionysus. Whom H. Jeremiah Lewis said, "Is the most Dionysian of them all (The Ptolemies)." Now I'm here though...

30. Trusting in the process of creating yourself through experiences, both light & dark and allowing your journey to take you where it may, will summon up favorable experiences and opportunities far beyond your expectations.

(Inspired By: My Dionysian Ways)

**It's better when your journey is the very embodiment of creating yourself, because when you try finding yourself, you become blinded by what you find. Not the finding of self, but the creating of self from life's experiences is like a beautiful inner journey that can help

you cross the inner rainbow to the treasures hidden within self.

31. Have caution of any society that only acknowledges one side of life, for when they only recognize one half of the world they begin to devalue the rest.

(Inspired By: New Age)

***New Age believers tend to only praise the Light and see Darkness as illusions. Do they not know that ALL life emerges from within the Darkness, whether it is a seed planted in soil, a baby born from the womb, or a star being birthed in the Dark Heavens which is surrounded by Dark Energy. As crazy as it sounds, to have faith without light, it is equally hard to imagine a world without Darkness. It's within our darkest times that the gods are nearest to us. I've learned things in the dark that I could never learn in the light.*

32. People spend their lives either complaining about the past or over analyzing the future. Therefore they miss the moment. People get so caught up in trying to seek their life's purpose or goal, when every person's purpose in life is to improve spiritually. And when I say spiritually, I mean Earthly.

(Inspired By: Living In The Moment)

**Do you know why people destroy the Earth without a care in the world? It's because their focus is on some far-off distant Heaven. They think whatever they do to the Earth means nothing, because this is not their home. Crazy because She(Earth) gives us everything we need— everything. Sounds like home to me.*

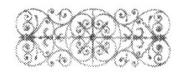

---

33. Names that have Sacred or Spiritual meaning to them are not who you are at the moment you receive the name, but rather it is an inner lighthouse on the path to who you are becoming.

(Inspired By: My Own Dionysian Name)

**Karneios Theones is my Dionysian title. Karneios is an ancient epithet of Dionysus, which means 'Horned Sun'. And being that my ancestors claim to be descendants of Dionysus, I spiritually feel that I am His Horned Son. As for Theones, it's an anagram of the old Greek word 'Entheos', which means a god within or inspired by god. Plus in the days of old 'Theo' meant god, so my name says there is a god within(Dionysus) and I'm inspired by the gods every time I'm in the mist of nature. I became 'Karneios Theones throughout my Dionysian journey. However, Theones is also related to 'Theoinos', which is another epithet of Dionysus which means Exhilarator.*

34. Sacred sex rekindles the torch of pleasure and the experience and emotions itself gives it strength to burn.

(Inspired By: Satyrs)

**Some ask why did I say Emotions? Because when dealing with Sacred sex, everything must come from within. Expose your inner depths, your darkest pleasures. For example... yeah yeah, I know... Imma keep it short. In my teens I had this secret foot fetish, and every time I fucked my girl I wasn't enjoying it, because I was hiding my true pleasure.*

Years later I met the right girl who was wild and free (like a Maenad). I told her my secret fetish and came to find out she loved women's feet as well. Once I was able to suck on her toes as I was making love to her, I suddenly became lost within the exchange. It became sacred sex, because I surrendered to my True nature. Be true to yourself, because nobody else will.

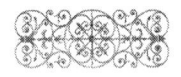

35. Life should not be a set of beliefs bound by restrictions, and forgiveness of sins based on salvation, yet life should be bound by life itself—a beautiful rejoicing that never falters during the experiences of life, no matter how dark it may get. Dark times are often times of growth and innovation.

(Inspired By: Maimakterion)

**Maimakterion is a Torchlight procession of feasts. Invitation to Dionysus Meilikhios (mild, gentle). Figwood Phallus rites of indestructible life. A life that can't be destroyed no matter how dark, actually Maimakterion was in honor of the nocturnal Dionysus. We celebrate this feast during the New Moon of November—a time to prune back the grapevines to leafless canes.

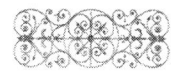

36. A foundation that's blueprinted off lies will only get built with bricks of deception. No matter what little truths of paint you add to the building, the structure and foundation will forever mirror the original blueprint.

They can stretch a lie so far by transmission that it doesn't enter the reality of truth, but share its similarities. However don't be fooled.

(Inspired By: The Bible)

**Don't be fooled by the Bible, because you see little truths in it. Most of its little truths are stolen twisted Pagan folklore.

37. Our individual destiny is not simply a gift or a curse projected by the gods or the Goddess, but a growth experience in the act of an immanent purpose. And the purpose is that as individuals we develop gradually

towards a better understanding of the divine that we humans naturally embody. Each individual is responsible for his or her own true nature and developing it fully, in harmony with the Earth.

(Inspired By: Self)

**Another person's gift may be another's curse. Let's not get caught up in gifts and curses and just enjoy our time here on Earth... Yeah I know what you're thinking. Do I not have gifts? No, absolutely not, whatever I'm good at comes naturally. If a lion kills a big-ass elephant, would you say the lion is a gifted fighter? No... Lions are natural killers when they want to be. Get my point?

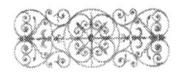

---

38. There's a unique beauty and freedom from fear when you understand that everything is cyclical—summer always follow spring. A butterfly from a caterpillar.

(Inspired By: The Seasons)

**Our solar system was birthed from the explosion of a star. We are here due to the cycle of life. So why shall I fear death? Nature shows me that nothing really ever dies, only changes form. And I'm okay with changing form, because I know nothing gets lost in the universe. Symbolically we must die off our old selves that no longer serve us, so to be transformed into our new selves,

our next cycle. The seasons show us this truth in a poetic way.

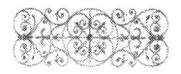

---

39. Existence in the natural world is an aspect or expression of the Goddess, gods or god you believe in or honor.

(Inspired By: The Great Goddess)

***"Together with the gods, I will tell of the birth of the elements which They personify," says Hesiod. This is surely true, because I'm sure Christians see the biblical god in everything just as Pagans see the Goddess in all things.*

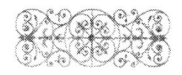

---

40. STREET JEWEL: Once you are aware of a man's deepest desires, you have exactly what you need to torment him.

(Inspired By: Desire)

***Desire-derived from the latin word 'de-sidere' (from a star). So to have desire means to be destined for the stars—a connection between human longing and the cosmos (Dark Heavens).*

No wonder desire feels heaven sent.

41. What the maggot calls the end of the world, Dionysus calls a Housefly.

(Inspired By: Dionysus Diphyes (two-natured))

**The maggot is what transitions to a housefly. Why is it that the transition of a caterpillar to a butterfly is more popular than the maggot into a housefly?
Do you not see the beauty in both?

---

42. Karma is a lesson to be learned through experience, not a revenge to be delivered.

(Inspired By: The Threefold Law)

**You can't dish out evil just because you think it's their Karma. She doesn't work that way. Her lessons come with growth and opportunities.

Back in school my PE teacher once gave me an F in gym because I refused to join the team prayer circle before the game. This really fucked with me because I felt he didn't respect my spiritual beliefs and plus it was wrong what he did, so I started plotting against him, because I knew his Karma was due. And at the time I was dabbling in the occult with my girlfriend. So I worked up a Karma spell on his ass.

I went as far as to steal his picture off his desk, wrapped it in black ribbon and herbs (can't remember which ones). And two weeks later I got kicked out of school and was hit by a car.

Karma ended up spanking me.

43. Existence is a privilege from nature, yet pleasurable living is a privilege from Dionysian wisdom.

(Inspired By: Earth & Her Mysteries)

***Dionysus the god is an initiate and priest of the Great Goddess Mysteries.*

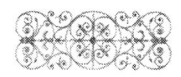

44. Experiencing the pleasure of nature and flesh is the ART of living a creative life that is graced with the presence of Dionysus.

(Inspired By: Ampelos)

***When Dionysus is in the mist, sex becomes more then sex. It becomes the act of giving yourself without holding back. Surrendering to Divine Passion(Dionysus) in His most erotic form. And knowing it's this giving that heals the other person, or gives them an experience like none other. It's a giving without expectation of anything in return.*

It's even better when there is the same giving from the other person as well. That's when it becomes a

Sacred exchange. Remember we get our word ' Orgy ' from the ancient Greek word ' Orgia '

---

45. If this society has no place for us Dionysian pagans, we will create one. Just as the Maenads and the Bacchants did in the days of old.

(Inspired By: The Maenads)

***The definition of ' Dionysian ' is 'wildly Pagan' and sensual. We use wildly Pagan in the terms of saying we belong to Nature, where we are free and at one with the wildwood. And we are sensual to the pleasures of Earth and flesh with Dionysus having a special place in our hearts.*

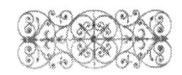

---

46. 'It seems that Aurics (ATD) tend to admire something in the spirit of Karneios Theones rather than his Dionysian words.On the whole they honor him for his creativity of such a positive tradition (ATD) of free love, freestyle rites and equality'.

(A comment left on my ATD website)

***ATD—Aurics Of Transcendent Divinity. A tradition I founded in 2013.Transcendent is used in the terms of the transcendent pleasures of Dionysus once He* *possess you through ecstatic dance, music, wine or sex. Auric is a modified short version of the word Auricle which means 'either atrium of the heart'. So, metaphorically, we are saying, "The Aurics are the Atrium of the heart of ATD."*

http://sirjohnatd.weebly.com/-blog/category/
http://auricdivinity.wixsite.com/theatd

47. It's stupid to think that the seeking of the Dionysus is the same for all, and to stress that there is only a single road to Dionysus, is to limit and take away from those whose journey needs other ways of learning and experiencing.

We are all differently fashion'd, so to create and bring forth different paths, so that All Dionysians may be able to seek Dionysus in their own way.

(Inspired By: The Mask of Dionysus)

***Someone once told me that my path (The Way Of The Satyr) was fairly new and only heard H. Jeremiah Lewis mention it once in his book, in which Jeremiah said, " ...is the way of the satyr. For these people, Dionysus is first, foremost, and in the end, a god of exuberance, joy, celebration, sex, drunkenness and reveling. Although they may be aware that there's more to the god, it doesn't really matter"*

Everything he said of us is absolutely true, until he said it really doesn't matter that there's more to Dionysus. Absolutely false, Dionysus Mask (Diverse Forms) means everything to us. And The Way Of The Satyr isn't fairly new at all. In the days of old they spoke on 'Dionysiacchoi Thiasoi Satyron', which roughly translates (Dionysian Priesthood of Satyrs). In these times we call it The Way Of The Satyr.

---

48. The Way Of The Satyr is a wild and simple Path that celebrates the chaotic joys and beauties of Nature and of being half animal/half human. It's about the wonderful experiences of Dionysus in all His forms. Praising the Mask itself...

(Inspired By: Komos)

**Komos—Satyr of festive banquets and the cup-bearer of Dionysus. However, there is no single right way to celebrate this path, all have value and all can inspire some new ways of experience.

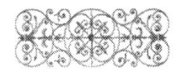

---

49. Your death, which is just a rebirth, is like a dead Fig falling from a tree, hitting the dirt so to fertilize the Earth, giving birth to a new Fig tree.

(Inspired By: Dionysus Sukites)

**Sukites is an epithet of Dionysus, meaning ' Of the Fig Tree '. As for Death—we've all been dead before. So, what's the big deal? Where do you think you were before you were in your mother's womb? Don't fear, we are just returning to the universal Mother's womb.

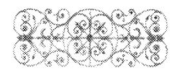

50. When it comes to the exchange of ecstatic bliss, if I could tell you what it is at its core, or what it meant, then there would be no point in fucking you... Shhh, just enjoy the mystery of the exchange.

(Inspired By: The Moment Of Bliss)

**Many times during my experience with sex, the female fucked up the moment by asking me how I do this, or am I good at this...? Blah blah blah.

Just let me do my thing and I'm sure I'll blow your mind. I'm a Dionysian. Sex is an art to us. Dramatic Arts.

Never ruin divine pleasure by trying to have strategy, just get lost within the ecstatic moment.

51. By observing or studying the shadows past of those we wish to curse, I'm sure we will find enough abuse, ache, and distress to make us stop wishing to curse them

even more. So, why not connect rather than hurting one another?

(Inspired By: The pain of my ex-girl)

*We are all fighting our own hardships, every last one of us.

As bad as I wanted to see my ex-girl suffer for giving up on me while doing my prison bid, it didn't equal the pain the outside world was raining down on her.

She was fighting a bigger monster than me, and most of the people we have issues with are fighting bigger monsters.

So, take it easy on them.

52. True loyalty is Full Circle, it's without beginning or ending. It's immanent. It's Dionysian.

(Inspired By: My Mother's Love)

*I remember when I was like three years old. It's a faded memory, but me and my moms were living in a shelter home. It never felt like we were homeless, because my mother's love overpowered the issue at hand. I felt safe with her by my side, even though we were truly hurting.

53. Evidence of the Goddess is sketched blissfully upon the Earths beauty.

(Inspired By: Gaea)

**Long Live Gaea..*

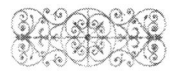

---

54. Immortality would diminish the precious time we spend on Earth, for it is death that gives life its purpose, and decay that fertilizes new growth.

(Inspired By: My own death to come)

**As for my own death, I want to be cremated. I want my family to take two handfuls of my cremated ashes to their backyard and mix it in the Earth's soil. And within that mixed ash soil, I want them to plant Apple (One of Dionysus sacred fruits) seeds there. So part of me can live within the Apple tree, as for when somebody tastes an apple fifty years in the future, they will be tasting an apple that was influenced to grow from my ashes. It is decay (Ashes) that fertilizes new growth.*

I also would like pinches of my cremated ashes tossed in fire during prayers as offerings to Dionysus. The smoke from my ashes will symbolize me taking their prayers to the Dark Heavens (cosmos). I want all this done in a ritualized fashion.

My cremation allows me to return as smoke to the swirling air, as fire to the Horn Sun, and as ash to fertilize the Earth. And if y'all hear about my death being any other way from this, please dig up my grave and give me my proper burial. I'll do it for you.

55. Committing your life to a single point of view (narrow vision) would make you easily exposed to error, or to be proven wrong in the end. So keep an open mind.

(Inspired By: Many Versions Of The Truth)

**My Dionysian Sister once took me to her mother's farm.

We walked over towards the cows and she bent down picking up something. She opened her hand in front of me and asked me what did I see? I said excitedly, "A Mushroom."

She said, "True, but I see Oracles from the gods."

At first I didn't understand, but that night we took them with the Honey mead she'd been cooking for forty-two days. The visions that invaded my subconsciousness were a true speechless experience. I saw a Mushroom, she saw Oracles—Two truths. Truths are diverse. Don't let anybody tell you different.

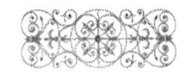

56. How we emerge from the world's dark experiences, the strength we gain from them, is what determines who we are. It truly depends on how we rise from the darkness that defines us as a person.

Doesn't a healthy flower depend on how it rises from the darkness of the Earth's soil before knowing if it's a good growth?

We mirror Nature, because we are all interconnected with Nature. If you look closely, She teaches us many lessons.

(Inspired By: Darkness)

*Good Wine can only be produced from soil that struggles.

57. Sometimes the Goddess of Love must play along with Daemons of mischief in order to at least earn their powerful tools (Hidden Wisdom) in their keeping. Does conflict not create positive change?

(Inspired By: Ancient Myths)

*If you must make this exchange with your own Daemon, you must not lose yourself within the process.
What I mean is, becoming the Daemon that you are facing. You must not lose sight that you are only playing around to gain their wisdom.

Now if you fuck around and become the Daemon, don't worry, because that only means you have been one, like me... Lol

58. Daemonic wisdom: Either embrace the Darkness or the darkness will embrace you.

(Inspired By: Dionysus Nyktipolos)

***My mother always wondered how I felt so comfortable sleeping in the woodlands alone at night at such a young age. I was always afraid to tell her, because I didn't think she would understand.*

It happened one night when I was twelve years old, when I was on a camping trip with my '4HClub.' I went into the woods at night and mentally reached out into the Dark...

After moments of silence, something reached back. Something ancient, a feeling I've never felt before. I'd made a connection with the wildwood. The soft, cool face of night asked me for a kiss (metaphor).

Now how could i explain this to a Christian mother?

Nykipolos is Dionysus as the "Night Prowler."

Oh yeah, calm down. When I say Daemon I'm not speaking on the Christian term demon. I'm speaking on ancient Nature spirits of the wildwoods, who enjoy the celebration of Earth and Flesh. Like Aglaea, Anteros, Philia, Gratia and Thalia, just to name a few.

59. The evil you cook up today you'll eat tomorrow!!!

(Trust me I know)

**I'm doing three life sentences plus 145 years, in a maximum security state prison.
So heed my wisdom on that.

60. Remain pliable enough to ebb amongst change, otherwise future growth is unfeasible.

(Inspired By: Growth)

**The Nature of all things is to change..

61. **STREET JEWEL**: Never constantly jab at your opponent's weakness, because then they may strengthen it.

Just save it as a chess move for times when you really need to checkmate the situation.

(Inspired By: Chess)

**Patience Predicts Prominence. I call this the Triple P'z. So, if you ever see my hands throwing up Triple P'z, I'm about to checkmate ya ass... Lol

62. Never allow the fears or desires of others to rule your actions.

(Inspired By: All My Weirdos)

**Be yourself, because everybody else is already taken.

I was once at a Starwood 28 festival in upstate NY, one of the largest magickal gatherings there is.

I went alone because I feared my homies wouldn't understand my spiritual life.

However, my homie Live (Goddess Bless his soul) followed me that day, because he thought I was sneaking off to commit a robbery.

After he ended up catching up to me and I explained the situation to him, he fully understood and we actually had fun.

My fear of telling him almost bypassed a beautiful experience, because two weeks later, he was killed.

So don't let fear stop you at all.

63. It's very simple, the quieter you become, the more you can hear.

(Inspired By: A finger to your lips... Shhhh)

**Give your ears the same opportunity you give your mouth.

At least be fair to yourself, because most of our worries are mere illusions, and I think if we silence them, sooner or later they will completely vanish.

64. We cannot have the wondrous journey of finding our path until we've lost our way.

(Inspired By: The Way Of The Satyr)

**Right when I thought all was lost, I found my path.

I had come to realize that getting lost was a part of my path as well.

It was the dawn of my path.

If it wasn't for me losing my way, I would have never thought I needed a better path in life.

In the process of losing my way, I found Dionysus... Like how Dionysus found the Goddess when He was lost to His madness.

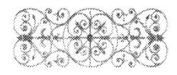

---

65. The fragrance of a female fresh out the bath (shower), is sweet and rich, like how the Earth smells after a day of spring rain.

(Inspired By: My Earthly Thoughts)

**The natural smell of my shorty (GF) reminds me of the Earth's fragrance.

---

66. Creating and following your own spiritual and Earthly principles is actually a sort of spell, not spoken or written, but expressed in your lifestyle.

(Inspired By: My Inner Book Of Shadows)

**Imagine how powerful a spell would be if it was all action and no words.

Remember you're the most powerful tool in magick. Become the embodiment of your spell.

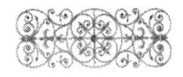

---

67. The force or spirit of Nature is to ebb and flow, changing from one thing to another, to stay fixed, or refusing to flow is to block the natural movement of life.

(Inspired By: The Phases Of The Moon)

**The same goes for us, if we fear change, we stop the natural process of growth. If we 'hold on' to our breath, stopping its flow, we will suffocate. So welcome change.

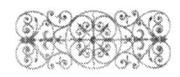

---

68. If you honor, respect and experience the pleasures of life, you would understand when Dionysus shares His ecstatic wisdom with you.

(Inspired By: My Foot Fetish)

**To be in connection with Dionysus, everything must follow its own natural bliss and pleasures.

I know you're thinking, "What's my own natural bliss?"

It's that pleasure you're shy about.

Yup, that one that arouses you like no other.

69. As a Dionysian Pagan, I treat the Dark times not as my adversary, but as a merit contender. So the darker things may get, the more strength I know I'm capable of accumulating.

(Inspired By: Dark Opponents)

**Don't ignore your hardships, or try banishing them. Battle them and gain your strength you deserve.

With no experience of living a full life, so to experiment with opportunities, the strength you have will remain dull and unused.

70. Love is too damn complex to be totally understood from a single point of view. Right? Or do we just make it that damn complex?

(Inspired By: My Diverse Love)

**The face of Love may change but the very substance of Her stays the same.

71. There isn't some Big guy in the sky per se, but the spiritual Nature of the Masculine force is like a Father to All.

(Inspired By: Zeus)

**No disrespect to Dionysus' Father. However, I always connected to the Earth gods, instead of the Sky gods....

Wow, that's crazy! As soon as I typed that I started choking real bad. I guess Zeus didn't like that comment or Dionysus didn't like me speaking on His Father.

Yet, what I said is true.

---

72. Create your own personal power and mold your own reality!

What if we choose to only live within the reality that we create, would that make us insane?

(Something to think about)

---

73. Celebrating and experiencing life in its full chaotic glory is better for me than whether or not a prayer gets answered, for faith is not mine to have. Yet experience is.

(Inspired By: Life)

**This is not to say that prayers aren't important to me, it's just I choose celebrating and experience over answered prayers.

Why? Because if one prayer gets answered, then every prayer should get answered. And just imagine if every prayer got answered.

That means the gods would be too reliable. And if the gods are too reliable, we'll miss Their greatest lesson—

Cherish life and all Her wonders.

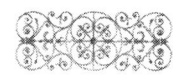

---

74. Our existence becomes meaningful once we cherish, honor, acknowledge, and merge with our own heart's desire, the gods expressing themselves as us through US!

(Inspired By: Rhythm of my heart)

***When we come to know who the gods are, They begin to tell us more about who we are.*

In many of the goddesses and gods, we can see reflections of ourselves.

---

75. Question—Is dishonesty essential when being honest is too perplexing to comprehend?

(Be Honest Now)

***In the year of 2001, summer time to be exact, I was sixteen years old and was deeply in love with this girl who never gave me a time of day. So, one night I had my Cult sister spending a night over my house. Told her* *about the girl I was deeply in love with. She asked me did I have a picture of her, which I did. She was my sister's best friend...*

Long story short, we ended up doing a love spell on her (which I don't recommend). Right in the middle of the ritual, my little niece walks in, candles and burning incense everywhere. She looked me dead in my eyes and asked, "Uncle John, what are you doing?"

I smiled and said, "Getting ready to pray."

I was dishonest, because being honest at that time would have been too complex to explain to a nine-year-old.

---

76. When something in others emerges from within because of you, be it inner beauty, or love or even wisdom, then you have made your first step towards the gods of antiquity.

(Inspired By: The Ptolemies)

***And I chant that my Dramatic quotes help to birth something from within y'all. I know at times, my quotes seem wild or Dark. However, then that's who it's for, the wild and Dark.*

My Dionysian wisdom isn't judgmental, it is for all. And, hopefully, when I'm gone, the future generations will quote me like how we quote the mad philosophers.

For example, I'm giving you a wild quote that inspired me growing up, and till this day I still quote him...

"If there were no god, it would have been necessary to invent him"
- Voltaire

This book is to leave my quotes and thoughts behind, in hopes that y'all quote me for generations to come, and if that's so, then just maybe I'll become immortal through those who quote me—a step towards the gods of antiquity.

Frank Palescandolo once said in his novel that, "Dionysus has taken refuge with the Muses. They draw on His divinity to give inspiration to artists of the world."

My quotes and adages that I give you within this book are drawn from His Divine Inspiration.

---

77. I fear that if I was to banish my negative emotions, my positive emotions would take flight as well. So I keep my balance intact.

(Inspired By: The Whole Of My Being)

***When I speak on the negative, I'm not speaking on evil. I'm speaking negative, in the terms of Anger, Hardship, Frustration and the Darkself (the deep self* *that we try to avoid, because we fear of what society thinks of that Darkself).*

---

78. To stress that something is sacred or special, is to express that you honor, cherish, respect, and value it for its own existence.

(Inspired By: Mother Earth)

**Do you honor, respect, cherish and value what you hold sacred for its own existence?
Sometimes we don't, especially when we take wild animals out of the wild just to domesticate them for our own entertainment.

---

79. The bodies of women provide our first experience of love, warmth and comfort. So to stand against women, then is to stand against life Herself. For they are the ones who bring life into this world.

(Inspired By: Every Woman there is)

**Like Councillor Mandizvidza said, "Women are the survival kit of the human race."
I have memories of how a friend of mine grew up without her mother, and then realized as a culture we are suffering that same loss and loneliness of love, comfort, a

positive feminine role model, nurturance, sense of connection and safety.

All because, as a culture we lived without a Divine Mother (goddess) for too long. The Earth as well provided humanity's first experience of Love, Warmth and Comfort.

We should be thankful.

---

80. The start-off point for many spiritual infrastructures are very interesting, yet they are rarely the most important feature of that foundation and its identity.

The fruits of that foundation are found not in its roots (start-off point), but at the end of its many branches and present manifestations.

(Inspired By: The Fruits of my labor)

****Just because a foundation was rooted in purity doesn't mean its future identity will remain pure.*
Measure a foundation by the fruits it bears.

---

81. True empowerment from within, is to have the capacity to construct your actions based on your own desires, values and sense of correctness, whether or not others approve.

(Inspired By: The Free Spirits)

**By following your own heart, you can encourage others to do the same. I was truly inspired to follow my own heart by 'Starhawk', a well-respected elder of the goddess' community.*

---

82. Your Mask tells people more about you than your actual self.

(Inspired By: Theater)

**What you're pretending to be can become your reality, so what does your Mask say about you?*
I can't answer that, because my Mask doesn't belong to me, it belongs to Dionysus.

---

83. If we try to shove away or abandon our own emotions, such as pain, rage, or fear, then we will not be able to accept those same emotions in others.

(Inspired By: Abandonment)

**How can you accept someone else's pain when you're running from your own?*

84. STREET JEWEL: Victory is when you allow your adversaries to believe that they are triumphant, until the end when they realize they are not.

(Don Honor)

**Bro, you may think you're Triumphant, because you're reading your own Book, but in the end you will realize that even your Book is no longer Author'd by you.*

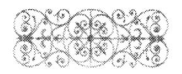

---

85. We should truly appreciate our reflection upon the surface of a Lake, Pond, River or Ocean, for it reveals a sacred connection between us and Mother Nature.

Seeing ourselves as we truly are within the beauty of Her creation. She's our mirror and we should mirror Her.

(Inspired By: The Mesopotamian River)

**A River which was named after one of Dionysus' Tigers, says an ancient 'aition.'*

86. At times my perception of life is similar to a phat kid in a bakery. I know exactly what to do, yet I don't know where to start.

(Inspired By: My Gramz Bakery Shop)

**I love you Granny, I'll see you in Summer Land, dancing on Mt.Nysa.*

87. One of the best spiritual aspects of growth is in the fact that Dionysus will not gaze upon your being for trophies, scholarships or awards, but for wounds of experience.

(Inspired By: Dionysian Experiences)

**The creating of Dramatic Art happens in very Dark (Wounded) places. Humanity was created from the heart of Dionysus along with the ashes of the Titans.

Due to the goddess Hera's jealousy, She sent the Titans (Elders gods-Chaotic forces) to kill the young Dionysus. The Titans ended up eating the young Divine child which angered Zeus to the point of destruction. He struck the Titans with His lightning bolts, turning them to ash.

In that ash, Dionysus' heart was recovered and with the mixture of the Divine (Dionysus) and the ashes of the Titans (Chaos) Zeus created Humanity. And this is why we are born with that balance of Divinity and Chaos.

We all have the very heart of Dionysus in us. Yeah, yeah, I hear. It's only a myth.

Know this though. As a Dionysian Pagan, it's not the myth that I believe in, but the gods in whom the myth helps us to understand.

Remember that!

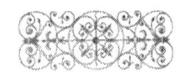

88. A wise Dionysian Pagan can create a beautiful dancing star from the chaotic energies that his enemies project his way.

(Inspired By: The stars I created)

*This book is one of the stars I created.

Many people sent a lot of chaotic energy my way during the creation of this book. Many doubted me, many said, "Nobody will ever be inspired by a prisoner."

Many called me broke, and that I'll never be able to afford an editor. Many said my education level is too low.

Blah Blah Blah... To all of y'all who spoke such BS, here's my Book, and yes, it isn't perfect, far from other educated books, but my god doesn't honor perfection or education. He honors life and experience.

Yes, I couldn't afford an editor, but that didn't stop my devotion to my god.

I did the best I could, and I chant that y'all are not disappointed in the many educated errors in this book.

My school was Life, the streets and the woodlands.

89. We can measure the heart of a woman by her connection to Earth.

(Inspired By: Dirt Worshippers)

***Within the Earthly carriages of women, the goddesses found each other. Women are channels for the goddess' love and passion.*

90. If there's at least one Witch within a community, that community then possesses a precious Moonstone.

(Inspired By: Moon, Stones and Witches)

**There's just this certain unique Aura that surrounds a Witch. As if their presence alone is magickal.*

91. In any Church in which a huge deal of worth is based on correctness, the people's true self will tend to dive under the bedcovers.

(Inspired By: Church)

**Just like a dog will forever have a portion of wolf in them, we as humans will always have a portion of the wildwood in us. And sometimes we need to allow that portion to run free.*

A sense of correctness has no place in what is natural to us. A part of your deep self belongs to nature.

Sometimes the more primitive we have to get, the more potent we are.

92. We all have our own truths, our own rituals and beliefs.

Dionysus has allotted many different aspects (Masks), so to speak to us in His own unique way. His enraptured love is all encompassing, He will present expressions that speak to all humans, no matter their age or race. So what difference does it make to stress over how a person seeks their own truth?

Why conform to fit the mold, when you have the tools to create one?

(Inspired By: The Mask Of Dionysus)

*I once met this girl whose spiritual belief was called 'Otherkin.' She felt that the very essence of herself was Wolf. No, seriously. She howled at every full moon, ran in a pack, and they actually had an Alpha Wolf.

One day they talked me into coming to one of their rituals. In the dead center of what seemed like a forest, we placed animal-fur jackets on, howled at each other, and inhaled this hallucinogenic herb.

Moments later the pack went wild and we started chasing each other, which they called the 'Other Hunt.'

At first this was fun and games to me, but as I chased them in the woods while howling, I actually started feeling my wild within responding to this ritual. I became a part of their truth, and actually felt the heartbeat of it.

When I caught my homegirl in the hunt and tackled her to the ground, I saw a look in her eyes that I'll never forget. She had the look of a wolf in her eyes. This was her truth. Nobody could change that.

This ritual opened my mind to the diverse truths that possess these lands.

93. You must learn to 'Be' and not to 'believe'. Not to analyze objectively, but to understand from within (wisdom of the body & heart). Don't have 'belief' in your existence, 'Be' your existence.

(Inspired By: My existence)

**It's like someone asking you, "Do you believe in the Air?"

No, we feel and experience the winds! So you must learn to feel and experience your existence, because belief implies doubt.

Life is here for the grabbing. No need for blind faith. You can see and touch Her (Life).

94. Fear and hardship are placed within your life to see how committed you are to your path. It's not the means of some devil, it's the means of growth, strength and courage.

(Inspired By: Common sense)

**God and the Devil at war is a Biblical creation story, and I'm not a part of that story. I'm of the goddess' creation.

Never went for that Devil story—no disrespect to my Luciferians.

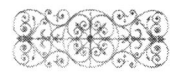

---

95. Never stress over what you have lost, enjoy and be thankful for what you have left.

(Inspired By: My ex-girl giving up on me)

**A wise person looks at what remains, and does their best with what's left.

---

96. Sometimes the things we want most will break apart, so that the things we need for growth can come together.

(Inspired By: Change)

**We have to destroy the soil (digging up), so to start the planting process for growth. Even Nature knows destruction (hardships) is the beginning of the growth process.

97. At times it is so easy for people to feel paralyzed by their daily life when they are unable to see a greater purpose.

(Inspired By: A higher purpose)

**If you want to see a greater purpose, look in the mirror.*

98. Some of the hardest decisions in life to be made are in knowing which characteristics to accept, and which ones to sacrifice.

(Inspired By: My Sacrificial Offerings)

**Which one can you sacrifice?*
And remember, sacrificing doesn't mean you're putting an end to its existence, you're surrendering it to your darker self.

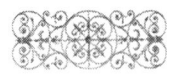

99. The most ancient and mysterious test that Dionysus gives us, is when He embeds a portion of Himself within us (His heart), and stands back to see if we ever become aware of the fact that He's always been a part of us.

(Inspired By: The Death of Zagreus)

**Zagreaus was believed to be Dionysus' first manifestation as the Son of the Underworld goddess Persephone, who, according to the Orphics, was elevated to the throne of Zeus, but who was then torn to pieces by the Titans, who cooked and devoured His body.*

Zeus, being extremely pissed at Their actions, punished the Titans by striking them with His lightning bolts which turned them to ash, and from these ashes, the human race was designed. So, it's only probable that our bodies are Dionysiac, if we were designed from the ashes of the Titans, who ate the flesh of Zagreaus (Dionysus), we are part of Him as well as those older gods (Titans) who were the children of Gaea (Earth).

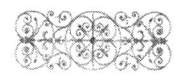

---

100. Majority of people must be transPLANTED first before they are able to flourish. Placing them within a darker area of soil, so to bloom much better.

(Inspired By: My Ivy Garden)

**Positive growth often requires a trip into the darker realms of self, or experience as part of the cycle of renewal, or growth.*

101. Don't ever forget that one of the chief Dionysian principals of life is to rejoice and celebrate it in all its diversity.

(Inspired By: Pyanepsion)

**The Pyanepsion are celebrations of The Harvest, The Grape Treading Dance, Masked Dionysian Rites & The Descent of Dionysus.*

In other words, it's like a Dionysian Thanksgiving, for in the days of old during this festival they gave Thanks to Dionysus for the Harvest. Even though Grapes played an important part in this rite, other fruits associated with Dionysus were harvested and celebrated at this time—such as figs and pomegranates. Both fruits are considered as symbolic of transition and initiation.

102. People tend to always lock themselves within one form of the Divine, therefore missing the beauty and experience of the other forms.

(Inspired By: The Gods)

**Dionysus is very well known for His many faces (Masks), and is often described by my ancestors as 'He of a thousand names.' Those names came with different forms. So I constantly remind myself not to get locked within only ONE aspect of Dionysus.*

Why would I when I can celebrate His many forms which bring so much color to my life. As the god of pleasure you can only imagine how I honor Him in such ways. Or as the god of Nature, walking within the woodlands inhaling His very essence. God of Theater—tearing up during beautiful plays or dramas, is honoring Dionysus, for He is who gave us Theater.

I can continue to go on, but I think you get my drift, it's better to honor All aspects of the Divine. For those ways mirror Life, because life is very diverse. However, the experience of 'contact with Dionysus' is different for different people.

Some will experience joy, others peace, some will laugh, others cry, some feel an inner vibration, others a quiet simple meaning, some will dance, make love and others will pray. Every one of these is equally valid to Dionysus.

Every Dionysian will find for themselves the Ecstatic way towards Dionysus and what may be the Ecstatic way for one may be completely wrong for another. So they follow the calling of their own heart and rejoice in that calling, and so shall you...

103. Dionysian Pagans don't attempt to hide from the mortal cycle of Life, Death and Rebirth. Our goal is to only explore and celebrate it.

(Inspired By: The Wanderer)

*Dionysus is also known as The Wanderer, Wandering the lands teaching the people of Winemaking.

To Wander is to explore. To explore is to celebrate what is found.

---

104. Celebrate your existence and you will see that your existence is interconnected to the whole of Life.

The seasons will mirror your mortal cycle, the birdsong will become your melody, Winter your death, and Spring your rebirth.

(Inspired By: The Cycle of Life)

**Each member of creation links into a web that in turn interweaves systems that interconnect magnificent patterns. From the tiniest microbe to the complex universe, everything is joined and actively works to maintain the integrity of its wholeness. And I celebrate this truth.

---

105. Have confidence in those who are seeking the gods. Question those who have found Them.

(Inspired By: An Oracle Visit)

**Majority of those who claim to have found the gods tend to try speaking for Them, which then brings in

manipulation. Key word 'Majority', I'm not saying All. So stop looking like that. You know there's truth to this, especially with my experiences with certain Oracles.

Remember this, when people don't quite understand the Divine, they begin to conjure up their own bias and in the process they create their own demons and devils to believe in.

106. It is impossible to prove by scientific means that Elemental spirits such as Satyrs, Nymphs and Faeries exist, for they are astral, metaphoric and spiritual in nature. However, this does not invalidate their existence.

The scientific community cannot provide a photo of an atom or an electron, yet they know these exist by the behavior of other substances around them. The same applies to the Elemental spirits of Fire, Water (Nymphs), Earth (Satyrs), and Air (Faeries). We know of their existence by the results we get when working with them, which affects our surroundings (around them).

(Inspired By: D. Conway)

***Hallucinogenic drugs are a part of our surroundings, here thousands of years before Humanity, they are helpers of the Elementals. The Earth provides us with herbs of healing and of inspiring. Magick Mushrooms open the eyes of the body, I'm speaking from experience.*

They actually call the hallucinogenic drug DMT the 'Spirit Molecule.' While on hallucinogens, I remember standing before a group of small Ivy leaves and asking, "Friends, speak to me of our Father Dionysus Kissos," and the Ivy leaves suddenly started to flourish.

---

107. At times it's our own mind that has complicated situations through its own wrong understanding and false notions. The only reason our spiritual path sometimes appears complex on the surface, is so that it can confront the harsh complexities of our ego and darkness.

(Inspired By: My Ego)

****It takes strength to overcome strength.*

---

108. My spiritual world mirrors my physical one, for all things are sacred in my eyes. I'm not seeking for salvation in some distant perfect place. I'm just enjoying the beauty of being at Home on Earth.

Dionysus gives me all that sustains me. However, just because I say all things on Earth are sacred doesn't mean that hardship, death and destruction are not as well. They are also sacred, because they play a part in the web of life.

(Inspired By: The Web Of Life)

**Life is what we make of it and it's up to us together (not some distant God), to create the Promised Land here on Earth for everyone.
We are responsible for our own destinies.

109. Menstrual Blood is part of the Divine, life-giving power of women, not a mark of sinfulness or uncleanliness as fearful patriarchal theologies have expressed. The word 'Ritual' comes from the ancient Sanskrit word 'Rtu' which meant 'menstruation,' and the ancient roots of the words 'menstruation', moon, mind, meaning and the name for prophetic Priestesses was all the same—'Menses'.

Actually, menstruation is what feeds the fetus for the first two months of gestation. So if it wasn't for the woman's menstrual Blood, as a fetus we wouldn't have made it through gestation.

Why would God mark that as the origins of sin? Sounds more like the origins of Life.

(Inspired By: The Life Blood Of Women)

**It's a fact that animals were on this planet millions of years before humans. So was the female animal's menstrual blood also a mark of sin from God? Hell No! The patriarchal men feared what they couldn't understand, so they marked something sacred as sinful.

Everything they say that comes from God was only them creating laws against a Religion they wanted to overthrow. The ancient Pagans saw sacredness in All Life, so they celebrated the power of women, of their menstrual blood, of sex, of nature. And whatever the Pagans celebrated, the patriarchal religions made it evil and sinful.

So, patriarchal laws weren't handed down by God, they were created out of jealousy and as a means to kill off a religion they stood against.

---

110. METAPHORICAL FAITH: It is certainly that when you jump off Mt. Nysa, you're either going to realize you have wings, or the fall won't be from so high up that it kills you. Or maybe it's just that, symbolically anyway.

When you jump off, even if the jump kills you, you have the power and strength to give birth to yourself again. I think the rebirth comes when you understand the purpose of the jump or fall.

(Inspired By: Dionysus Psilax)

**Psilax is the winged aspect of Dionysus.

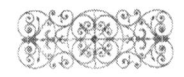

111. This may sound harsh, but suffering also has its place. It's one of the important ways in which we grow.

At times we must allow others to suffer, using our understanding wisely, when it is truly needed or when it will not derail someone from the path they need to experience.

If we do not have this wisdom, it is best not to interfere.

(Inspired By: Purposeful Suffering)

*If I never suffered, I wouldn't have known how deep my mom's love was for me. And now that I know how deep it goes, that love drives me every second in life.

112. A promise is a reflection of the person who gives the promise, not the one accepting it. And if that promise is ever broken, it takes something away from that person. Like a metaphoric amputation—you're still living, but something is now missing.

(Inspired By: Blood Promises)

**You may think, 'No, a promise isn't that in depth'. But remember I'm speaking from experience and plus I'm talking about Blood Promises to the gods. I once made a Blood Promise to a deity on the night of the Blood Harvest Moon. I will not give the name of the

deity, for I believe She is still in some ways upset with me.

Long story short, due to greed, I broke the promise. Actually, I had forgotten about the promise. But as soon as my actions broke such a promise, I immediately felt something within me die. Suddenly visions of the promise invaded my mind. It brought tears to my eyes and for the next two years I gave burnt offerings, with a little blood since I gave blood during the promise.

So, now do you understand the inspiration of the quote?

---

113. The reality of Dionysus as a Whole to His many diverse Masks (different forms), makes plenty of sense, if you consider that the Whole may need all of Himself, so to fully experience Himself.

(Inspired By: Dionysus Polyonomos)

***Just as we need our whole brain so to fully and correctly experience ourselves, mirrors Nature (Dionysus Polyonomos). The whole needs all its details in order for it to be a whole. And Polyonomos is an epithet of Dionysus that means Many Named.*

Question—Where would the head get its power, if not for the Whole?

114. Even the worst deaths are not deaths at all, it's just a brief transformation which is followed by a new birth in one form or another. And with that said, rest easy and know that nothing gets lost in the universe.

(Inspired By: Nature)

***Life and Death are not separate forces, but are different aspects of the same Entity (Dionysus).*

H. Jeremiah Lewis told Dionysus within his poetry, "You have torn me to pieces and built me back up in your image." This statement is the very heart of being a Dionysian in my eyes. Allowing Dionysus to destroy us within His madness just to ecstatically create us in His Divine image. The heart of initiation into The Ways Of The Satyr.

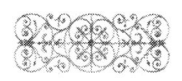

115. Life is abandoned if it's not lived as a celebration.

(A Satyr's Proverb)

**I tend to not seek a 'Motive' for this world, I only attempt to experience & honor the wonders of this world. And I even see wonders in chaos.*

116. The universe is surely alive and is aware of my experiences. The proof is within my mysterious dreams

in which I feel more awake than asleep, where the universe comes to me like a mother's encompassing embrace.

(Inspired By: My Dream)

**This a dream I had on 3/31/15 (I was outside with my father and cousin in New Jersey, 'My birthplace', when we saw the moon in the night's sky. It was so close as if I could hit it with a rock. It was extremely huge and I could feel its gravitational pull within my body, yet it felt more like a hug. It was so beautiful and scary at the same time (Dionysus is the unifier of opposites).*

Suddenly the moon had grown into an orange color, then burst out three fireballs onto Earth where we were. The first two died out, and the last one burst into a small group of birds that flew everywhere.

---

117. In molding our own reality, we become the form we create. We merge into the energy that we summon up. So, mold responsibly!

(Inspired By: Idolatry)

**The gods gave us the very 'Tools' to mold our own reality. They are called 'Freedom' and 'Imagination'. The reality I have molded is a very metaphoric journey, and during my journey of life, I tend to always go on a date with Darkness, accept a dance with Fate, have a drink with Pleasure, leave with Joy, have sex with

Karma, fall asleep with Hardship, wake up with a hangover of Wisdom, and suddenly, realize I'm living in my Earthly home of Self.

The Earth is full of beauty. However, the greatest beauty of it all is the Sun and Moon that radiates from the heart. Don't be afraid to let people see it rise. We are Nature personified in the forms of human flesh.

---

118. The chants and wonders of our ancient Pagan ancestors turned soil into terracotta, terracotta into figurines, figurines into goddesses, and goddesses into Women.

(Inspired By: My Ancestor Cleopatra)

**Cleopatra was a descendent of The Ptolemies, who my Gramz says are my ancestors, even if it's just through the fact that the Ptolemies both gave me my middle (Phillip), and last name(Auletta).

---

119. People know within their hearts that when they truly fall in love, the world suddenly becomes full of magick and wonder.

What they fail to realize is that when they discover the universe being full of magick and wonder, they fall in love with the world.

(Inspired By: Worldly Pleasures)

** When I speak on magick, I'm not speaking of stage magic. I'm talking about the magick in Love, Sex, Ritual, Dance, Beauty, Music, and Self. This is the type of magick that fuels our Land, you should honor and celebrate it. Unaware development for magick is deeply buried within us all, we must dig deep and conjure it to the surface.

---

120. Hardships are Opportunities. In overcoming them, we give ourselves strength and character, insight and compassion. They are the means by which we take form.

(Inspired By: My Prison Bid)

** This may sound crazy, but being sent to prison has opened up many opportunities. Being locked in a cell for twenty-three hours a day has forced me to look within. And within yourself holds many opportunities, insight and compassion.

Many ancient Prophets have been to prison including Dionysus. When Pentheus arrested Him and His Maenads, which gave insight into how powerful Dionysus was. His influence just by His beauty. Something that was hard for Pentheus to deny.

121. Dionysian Pagan myths are not mere stories, but mirrors of the great cosmic drama of seemingly impersonal forces. They also become metaphors that enable us to see our own personal stories reflected in their archetypal patterns.

(Inspired By: Euripides)

**Our ancestors created ancient myths to explain reality in their own unique way, making creation conscious of Herself. For example: The myth of the departure (descent to the Underworld) and annual return (returning to Earth) of the Greek goddess Persephone (Dionysus' first mother), is an explanation of the changing seasons. Her descent is Winter, and Her return is Spring. (Same for my All Father Dionysus).

Some myths were attempts to explain natural phenomena, so to bring us closer to nature. However, the crucial point was not to become so attached to one's own myth, one's own path, in failing to understand the validity of other myths and paths. Like how the Bible and Quran does. They fail to understand the validity of other myths and paths.

---

122. If your beauty and power radiates so great and bright that nobody can see through it, the love then becomes an illusion. Because if love is offered, it's only

offered to the beauty and power, never to the Woman behind it.

(Inspired By: Ariadne)

**How can you love something when you only admire some of the details of the WHOLE? To truly love, you must love All the details that make up the WHOLE. A person's Beauty is only one detail of that person. Yet, what are the details that make up that Beauty?*

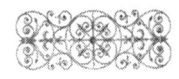

---

123. INITIATION QUESTION (From The Way Of The Satyr): Is it possible to Want and Fear something at the same time? Can you Fear what you Want with the same intensity? How or Why?

(Inspired By: Mystery)

**I would give you my answer, but then that would influence yours, and that I don't want to do, for this moment is yours, not mine.*

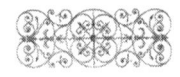

---

124. I see the Goddesses and Gods composed of energy, as energy shaped by human attraction, attention and experience over many thousands of years. Do They have faces? To us Dionysians, They do. Maybe They know that-that's how They have to communicate Themselves

to us. They have to be understandable within our reference.

However, I see Them also as projections from ourselves (imagination), for we are a part of the universe too and so are They.

(Inspired By: I see myself through Their eyes)

**Aleister Crowley once said in his Gnostic Mass, "There is no part of us that is not of the gods." I truly agree!!!*

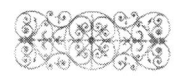

---

125. As soon as a spark of Nocturnal Light, or a Creation of Beauty is glimpsed, it is taken over by those whose mission it is to pervert and exploit it, to the extent of transforming what is beneficial into something maleficent, which is exactly what happened to Dionysus and His ecstatic blessings.

(Inspired By: #WeGotHisIvyNow)

**You can call us whatever, Neo-Dionysians, Neo-Satyrs, or Neo-Maenads... it doesn't matter. Just know that we are His descendants and here to challenge your Humanity!!!*

---

126. Don't exist only to live for yourself, because if you do, you'll be cursed with the constant boredom of your

own ideas and views. We are created to be social and helpful creatures, for the hands that help are more sacred than the tongues that speak prayers.

(Inspired By: Helpful Hands)

*** Our ideas and views tend to expand through our encounters with people. Imagine if those encounters stop.*

127. Your Mission doesn't become beautiful until your work mirrors the heart, Nourishes the mind, and caresses the senses.

(Inspired By: Dionysian Art)

*** Ask yourself that before taking up any Mission. Would this Mission or Goal mirror my heart? Would it Nourish my mind? Or even caress my senses? Don't think Missions shouldn't bring us pleasures. All things in life should have a pleasing aspect to it.*

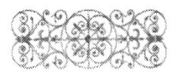

128. By learning to walk and live in Balance, you can keep your life from being dominated or seduced by any extreme.

(Inspired By: Karneios)

*** This is a 'Proverb' for The Way of the Satyr.*

129. Compared to the Earth Herself, our lifespan as humans is mighty short, and it would be an offense against Nature (Dionysus) for us to take the world's crisis so seriously and dignified that it puts us off from enjoying the things we are presumably designed to enjoy in the first place. Like: The opportunity to fall in love, to make Babies laugh, make ecstatic love and to enjoy the company of friends, lovers and family.

(Inspired By: Dionysian Law)

*Celebrate Life is our Law. Celebration provides us with a sense of connection that underlies sacred reality, of being at one with Nature and the Body.

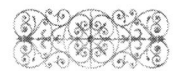

---

130. The word 'Scorn' derives from the Italian word that meant 'without horns', for to be without Horns was a sign of shame, disgrace or contempt. The ancient horn gods and goddesses were revered, respected and honored by our ancient Pagan ancestors. Their horns represented Their power and connection to Nature and animal life, which was held sacred in the days of old.

The Germanic 'Gott' and English word 'God' come from an Indo-European root word 'Go', which means 'The Bull'. In ancient times the Bull was a sacred animal to many horn gods, such as Dionysus and Pan. And sometimes They took the form of the Bull. So when one speaks of 'God', they are really secretly honoring Dionysus and His sacred Bull.

(Inspired By: All The Horn Deities)

***There are a lot of Scornful people out there, they should learn to grow their Horns. Do you proudly show yours?*

131. Just imagine how intoxicated the melody of the universe would be if humans had not lost the power to listen with their hearts and hear the song of Dionysus, which echoes the rhythm and desires of the human heart.

(Inspired By: The Frenzy)

**Every time I felt like the stress of the world was too much to bear, I'd go buy a bottle of wine. Go to the nearest woodlands and find the one spot that sang to my heart. Take my shoes and socks off so that I also felt the rhythm of Dionysus.

I'd sit my back to the tree and take a deep breath inhaling everything the tree had to give me. Pour out an offering, while just sitting there getting lost to the beauty of Nature. This is the key to hearing Him...

"If you truly wanted to hear His melody, you'll find ways to hear it." Just find YOUR way!!!!

132. Is it not Awe-Inspiring how women have the ability to conceive a new human life, give birth, produce milk and to bleed with the phases of the moon. She alone has the power to produce and nurture life. Without her, new life would perish. Women and Nature share the great role of Motherhood which is a biological fact. So to me 'women' or should I say 'womoon' and Nature are the closest expression or form to the Divine.

(Inspired By: AD & His Wifey)

**"We should never forget that the Dionysiac world is, above all, a world of women. Women awaken Dionysus. Women accompany him everywhere wherever He is"

Frank Palescandolo (Phallos Dionysus).

133. In life many things are NOT ' either-or ', but rather BOTH. And it's our job to find a beautiful balance between the two (Both).

(Inspired By: The Nocturnal Light)

***Just like there's a little Darkness in All Light, there's a little Light in All Darkness. True story, because I'm sure there's a little Light within the depths of my inner underworld where my Daemonic aspects rest. Give me some beautiful things that your Daemon has done?*

134. A life that is enrich'd in Love, Pleasure, Risk, Friendship, and Adventure is always better than a secure one. Take chances, dare things, get messy and make connections and more likely unusual events that lead to beautiful experiences will fall into your lap.

(Inspired By: Ecstatic Love)

***Love that doesn't expect risk, messy mistakes or chaotic growth aren't worth the effort of giving or accepting. At least not to us Satyrs.*

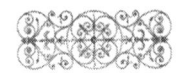

---

135. I think another wise phrase should be added to the ancient Apollo Admonition saying of 'Know Thyself'. In these modern times, we should add 'Accept Thyself'.

(Inspired By: Me—Karneios)

**I think it's important to Accept who you truly are before trying to conform to another's spiritual path.

People must learn to Accept and befriend all the states of themselves—both male and female, light and dark—in order to be truly whole.

Apollo shared a Temple with Dionysus, so ' Accept Thyself ' should be placed on Dionysus's side of the Temple.

136. At times we need to give ourselves permission to be Ecstatic, to feel love and to experience Pleasure again. And to be strong and wise enough to comprehend that all life, of hardships and failures, as well as the gifts and blessings from Dionysus are cyclical by Nature. So enjoy the moment while you have it!!!

(Inspired By: The Moment)

*Jean S Bolen, stated in her Gods in Everyman, "A Dionysus man exists in the present, which is the only reality for him." This is absolutely true—for I am summoned to whatever intensifies my experiences in the moment.

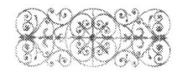

137. It seems like this world doesn't have enough Religion to make us love one another, no matter the differences, yet it has just enough religion to make us KILL and HATE one another for our differences. What does this tell you?

(Inspired By: Christianity)

*It's beautiful to seek a spirituality that opens the mind, rather than one which seeks to narrow it.

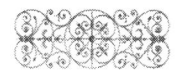

138. When eating the grapes of Dionysus ecstatically, the Vine silently makes His mystery known to those who are willing to listen.

(Inspired By: Staphylos)

**Staphylos is the embodiment of the Grapes. Actually, He is one of the sons of Dionysus. How you're willing to listen is completely up to you, yet listen wisely, because The Vine speaks madly!!!*

139. The Dramatic Arts is like Love. It's embedded within us all. It only takes us to look deep within so to recognize what our Dramatic Arts are. In that case I guess we shall call them Dionysian gifts. Gifts that we are All born with since we All contain a portion of Dionysus's heart.

(Inspired By: Universe)

**Even the Universe knows this, pay attention to the first three letters of 'Universe'. U-N-I There's a message there. She's telling us we are in Her.*

140. Never under any circumstances take an ecstasy pill and a Viagra on the same night. Because you're going to have one Hell of a HARD time.

(Inspired By: My own mistake)

****I'd just met this beautiful shorty. She radiated like The Great Aphrodite. I knew deep inside if I was to have sex with her, I'd be so excited that I wouldn't last over five minutes without releasing my blessings (And I'm pushing it with five). So, I took an ecstasy pill and a half Viagra, then took her to the hotel. Oh my Goddess, this was the BIGGEST and HARDEST mistake of them all. My Phallus was hard and throbbing for six hours straight. It went from the best sex ever to a crucial migraine in both heads. Surely Dionysus's son Priapus was proud.*

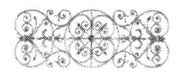

---

141. Symbolically, the Mask of Dionysus Lampteros is like a lighthouse to a ship at sea. He tells me where the shore is, where the rocks lie, offering guidance in a storm or on a dark and starless night. But, ultimately the decision as to how I chart my course is my own. Do I sail or motor, tack, or run for a long haul? Do I head for the port, or push on? My choices, my free will, my expectations, fears, longings and beliefs all affect the outcome of events. And within this truth, my truth, I find strength, courage, love and growth from making my own choices and learning from them.

(Inspired By: Free Will)

***Dionysus Lampteros in the days of old embodied the Torch-Bearer... Depending on what path you choose, you can either Survive or Thrive!*

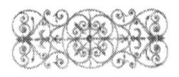

---

142. By our own actions and choices, we can change our life. We are not Prisoners or Slaves of Fate, but are an integral part of it. We can grasp the web of Fate and beautifully weave in our own special, sacred, personal pattern. However, be aware, because being able to weave our own destiny comes with responsibility.

(Inspired By: The Moirae)

***If you don't like the life you were born to, you have the power to weave your own. However, your own creation will still bear hardships... That's The Fates' way of growth. If you're in fear of taking any chances of molding your own life, I swear you chance even more!*

---

143. If you wish to go back to your ordinary life after encountering Dionysus, I symbolically suggest you to never make love to Him or drink from the Wine He offers.

(Inspired By: Grapes)

** "Like the god Dionysus, he may wander through many places, attracting women to him, disrupting their normal lives, and then moving on." Jean S Bolen

As for me, Dionysus has disrupted my life in a beautiful way and hasn't moved on yet. I guess He fell in with me, my flesh and the experience felt familiar to Him.

---

144. People who deny the pleasures of life are like rude visitors at a swingers party that's given by the sexiest hostess of all.

Among the ecstatic movements, diverse desires, beautiful fetishes, lovemaking, Dionysian music, wine and a variety of wonderful people, it is extraordinarily rude to sidle away and just say no.

(Inspired By: Soma)

**The gods gave us beauty and pleasure to be appreciated, it feels good to our senses for a reason. Why question what the gods gave us?

---

145. Ideas are like flowers, they need patience and many sets of conditions before they can flourish.

(Inspired By: My Fertile Mind)

**I've learnt this the hard way, even though I'm the type to live in the moment. There are things that just need growth and nourishment. And ideas are one of them.

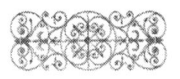

146. Not only has Mother Earth given us the gift of life, but also the means to survive, a way to protect our purposes. She has not abandoned any bird, human, plant or animal, to live in a Dionysian environment without the means to survive.

Mother Earth gave all living creatures a way to protect themselves: Claws, thorns, fangs, camouflage, speed, human intelligence to create ways of protection, acute senses of vision and hearing. This should tell you that we all have a purpose, for She gave us all ways in which we can protect those purposes.

(Inspired By: Protection Spells)

**However, gifts that are abused only turn into Karma that must be paid. Allow your gifts to be natural, don't manipulate it. Use your gift of protection to protect Her (Mother Earth), for She truly needs it.

147. When a person "tames" you or "domesticates" you, then that person loses that part of you which attracted them to you to begin with. Then you lose yourself in the process.

(Inspired By: Pan)

**Never abandon yourself to become a copy of another. Remain wild and free (Dionysian).

148. If you are looking for a life-changing experience, go through a life changing hardship. Enjoy!!!

(Inspired By: Life)

**Prison is my life-changing experience. It's a tearing apart that Dionysus felt was necessary. Yup, He destroys those He loves so that He can recreate You in His image. It's a mirroring of His myth and I am honored to mirror such a Dramatic myth.*

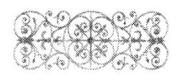

149. Once the first kid is birthed, the mother is also born. She never existed before the first kid. The woman existed, but never the mother. So the first kid brings two births.

(Inspired By: Diana, Goddess of Childbirth)

**What a beautiful process.*

150. Telling a big enough lie, in time, will become somebody else's belief.

(Inspired By: The Bible)

**People would easily believe a likely lie before an unikely truth.*

---

151. Huge opportunities to help people rarely presents themselves, yet small opportunities encircle us every day. If it's impossible to help many, at least help one. We're not here to see through one another, but to see one another through. It is a human instinct to help, for caring is a reflex.

(Inspired By: Instincts)

**If one was to slip, watch how quick your arm goes on to help. Exactly, it's natural.*

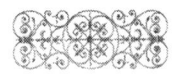

---

152. Ladies and Gentleman, please never get it twisted. When it seems that a Dionysian is getting lost within the bliss of lovemaking, it isn't he/she who is causing such pleasure, it is Dionysus himself.

(Inspired By: Dionysus)

**Those who commune with pleasure invoke Dionysus.*

153. People tend to think a rabbit's foot brings much luck, yet, however, that same luck you are depending on didn't work for that rabbit, now, did it?

(Inspired By: Dionysus's Midwife Hermes)

**And know this—true luck never gives freely, it only loans out. Sounds wild, but it's true... All truths bear a form of Darkness. If you don't believe me look up past the skies and tell me what you see.*

154. I don't want to just live the length of my life in celebration, but also live the length of my life in love and pleasure. I want to live full circle, to the point that the universe becomes aware of my existence.

(Inspired By: My Dionysian lifestyle)

**If you don't live life, you risk life living you. And trust me, She is chaotic in her living.*

155. Just because I am a man that lives a diverse lifestyle, or should I say many "double lives", doesn't make me a liar. I am just a man of many truths. I am very spiritual, yet also street. Very humble, yet also dangerous. Very faithful, yet also polygamist. Very dark, yet also a spark of light. Very earthly, yet also cosmic.

(Inspired By: The masks of Dionysus)

**Every mask I wear has its own truth.*

156. Darkness is similar to magick. It's an energy that is neither good nor bad in itself, but rather takes its quality, its moral coloring, from the way it is being used or looked at.

(Inspired By: The Nocturnal Sun)

**Darkness is what you make it. Now doesn't that sound dark? lol.*

157. If you can't keep up with the pace of your friends or family along the path they are traveling, perhaps it is because you hear a different calling. So, go instead where there is no path and leave your tracks.

(Inspired By: The Wind)

**Embrace the call of your ancestors.*

158. If you have ever lost a loved one, be it a family, friend, or homie. The bittersweet tears are summoned by the memories of moments when you have loved not enough. So, love fully during every moment.

(Inspired By: D.I.P Dice)

**Every time I think of my homie no longer being here with me, thoughts of all the things I could have done with him invade my heart. Wishing every day that I could have loved him more.*

159. People tend to observe the world in the wrong manner and then have the nerve to say that the world has misled them. You must only change your perception so you can see things as they are. To be as you are...

(Inspired By: Dionysian Blessing)

*** The blessings of Dionysus are joy and passion, madness and prophecy, ecstasy and freedom. Dionysian freedom is beyond good and evil. It takes precedence over law, custom, inhibition or morality.*

In the worship of Dionysus, we discover who we really are, beneath all the masks and lies and compromises that society demands of us. Dionysus dissolves all boundaries and destroys every falsehood. In the ecstatic state, we feel ourselves to be whole, to be one with all of the other worshippers, with the earth and the Gods. We utter prophecies, since we are no longer constrained by our small minds. We perform miracles, since the laws of nature no longer apply.

We touch the Mask of god, and He touches us.

160. STREET JEWEL: The mental stagnation of a disloyal person, is not that he cannot be loyal, but that he cannot believe anybody else to ever be loyal.

(Inspired By: Loyalty is Everything)

**My ex-girlfriend always accused me of being disloyal, to the point that it actually drove her crazy. If a girl talked to me for over five minutes, she'd swear I was cheating. These heavy accusations only ended up exposing her disloyal nature. I laughed at the situation, because for one I always knew of her ways. I never tripped about it, because I'm a firm believer in sharing the pleasures of life. It was her own rules that ended up driving her crazy.

---

161. The sacred core of the journey exists within the journey. The seeker who is looking is themselves the sacred core of the journey. So, to find any truth you must first take that journey within and then you will realize that your own personal goddess/god dwells within you, as you.

(Inspired By: A Satyrs Journey)

**Be a beacon of your own truth, for YOU are your own truth.

---

162. The work that takes the most effort out of us, is the same work that usually nobody gets to see or know about.

(Inspired By: The Power Behind The Throne)

**I write for those whose quotes have never been read.

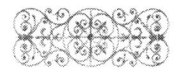

---

163. A rumor or gossip needs not be false for its essence to be evil. It could be a nasty truth that was forbidden to be passed around.

(Inspired By: K.J Bible)

**Exodus

---

164. Negative people are always caught off-guard when finding out that positive people can be more clever.

(Inspired By: The Sphinx)

**There's more that meets the eye, even the Eye Of Horus.

---

165. The sense in fragrances of the different seasons, are in its core, the emotions of the Earth. In spring She's enthusiastic, in Summer, She's in love, Fall She's concerned, and in Winter She's Furious.

(Inspired By: Semele)

**Dionysus' mortal mother Semele, was once worshipped as an Earth Goddess. In the language of the Phrygian inhabitants of Asia minor, the word Semele means "Earth."

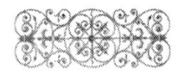

166. The truth remains, so whether you agree with it or not, the truth is your own experience, it cannot be captured by an idea or concept.

(Inspired By: Consciousness)

**You are more than an idea or concept.

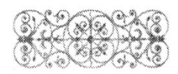

167. For all my elders, do not see them as wrinkles. Think of them as evidence of wisdom and proof of long experiences from living a full life.

(Inspired By: Gramms)

**I can say with all confidence that my Gramms is the wisest person I've ever known. You can hear it in her voice when she sings. Don't believe me, listen to her song

168. Has anyone ever seen or experienced a god/goddess that is not a portion of oneself? Do we not possess the Love of Aphrodite, the Wisdom of Athena, the Pleasure of Dionysus or the Strength to make sacrifices for a better perception like Woden?

(Inspired By: The Divine)

**The gods/goddesses are within us all.*

169. As a Dionysian pagan, my aim is to always intensify the pleasure of the mysteries: "For it is better that you rush upon this blade, than to enter this Earth pleasureless."

(Inspired By: Teletarches)

**Teletarches is also a name used for Dionysus, meaning the lord of initiation.*

170. Your ability to think is the most powerful expression of free will. perhaps you cannot control what happens to you, yet you CAN control what happens IN you. What you think will determine your experience of how it affects you.

(Inspired By: Meditation)

**If you do not practice your ability to think for yourself, then the mind has no choice but to mechanically think as it has been previously "trained". In this way you repeat the same mistakes and act according to the same misconceptions over and over.*

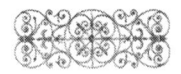

---

171. In sharing my story and experience of the goddess/gods and ancestors, I share their story as well, continuing their memories. I make a connection in which I bind the past.

(Inspired By: Pagan Mythology)

**To bind is to be bound. I am the retinue of Dionysus.*

---

172. Those aiming for some perfect distant paradise, often lose sight of the Earth and Her sacredness.

(Inspired By: The Biblical Heaven)

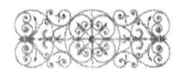

---

173. We must not be afraid to be outdone nor to face our fears, or the next generation will cease to learn.

(Inspired By: My Ancestors)

174. Beauty, love and pleasure, come at moments of living your ecstatic truth. It's when you are most trusting and authentic and feel that whatever you are doing, which can be quite ordinary, is simply sacred.

(Inspired By: The Muses)

**The Muses actually taught Dionysus His inspirational art in music, song, and dance.*

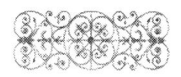

175. A glass of champagne in the hands of a beautiful woman... is like a well-intrigued poem.

(Inspired By: My Opinion)

**I know that all women are beautiful and sacred.*

176. Dionysian wisdom is never dogmatic. It learns from all. He's diversely universal in His ways.

(Inspired By: The cult of Dionysus)

**Wisdom is not hidden but often ignored. Open yourself to see more.*

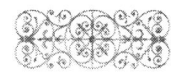

177. He who denies the dark, denies personal growth. He who denies Madness, denies life. Such a person will find neither life pleasurable, nor Madness easy to bear.

(Inspired By: Ishtar)

***People's conformed understanding of the chaotic nature of Dionysus is that it is (eventually, anyway, as seen through the eyes of a non-initiate) complete madness. The beautiful result is liberation, and thus, being better able to fully express and understand one's nature, but the path to get there involves at least temporarily completely losing yourself in Dionysian madness, just letting go completely. There is no control, and the point is perhaps to lose control. There is almost no self in it at all, just ecstatic frenzy. The frenzy I fell in love with.*

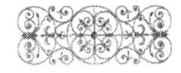

178. Be true to your own understanding and turn away from those things which oppose the good in you or are harmful to you.

(Inspired By: Italian Witchcraft)

**One of the convenants of Aradia

179. Most people would be surprised to learn that many things seem true only because they believe them to be true.

(Inspired By: Maat)

*What people think and believe determines what they experience and perceive.

180. Your character is your destiny. By changing your character, your habitual attitudes, beliefs and actions, you change out your destiny.

(Inspired By: Clotho)

*People are characters of their own making. However the price of change is sacrifice.

181. A positive attitude and a true desire to get well composes at least eighty-five percent of all healing processes.

(Inspired By: Mom Dukes)

** Keeping a positive and happy mind will help to strengthen your willpower to fight off any sicknesses you may encounter.

182. Take to be true your victory, even if there is none, because by assuming the ambiance of victory, you gain the victory itself, for you are the manifestation of your own truth.

(Inspired By: Nike)

**You cannot act as you don't feel.*

183. Live freely without regrets, because all things have their purpose for occurrences. You can only reconstruct your future way of thinking and extend your efforts to improve in a manner to uphold what is genuinely righteous.

(Inspired By: Ragnar Lothbrok)

184. The world only sees what they can comprehend. They can't understand what lies within.

(Inspired By: Lily Of The Valley)

**This is why it is so hard for this society to accept that the gods/goddesses are within as well as without.*

185. If you are in any doubt about why you exist, then you are not living. Celebrate your existence and within that celebration, I am sure your doubts will fade away.

(Inspired By: Slip)

**Enrich all that life is. Dionysus had the power to inspire and to create ecstasy, and his cult had special importance for art and literature. Performances of tragedy and comedy in Athens were part of two festivals of Dionysus, the Lenaea and the Great (or City) Dionysia. Dionysus was also honored in lyric poems called dithyramb. So honoring Dionysus in poetic form is a very ancient practice.*

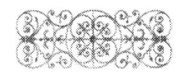

186. A child is conceived through pleasure but is delivered in pain.

(Inspired By: My Birth)

*ced="left"*Can you not see the Dionysian balance in all things? Even though Mom Dukes said I popped right out. I guess the hell I put her through makes up for my painless birth. Sorry Mom.*

187. We never gain our true strength from the things which are familiar or positive, but gain it within the facing of our fears within shadows or within our refusal to change.

(Inspired By: The Madness)

**Many may think otherwise, however within my experience this is true. Those who are Mad will agree with this, for what's familiar to us is just that, familiar. Face your deepest and darkest self and see the strength I'm speaking on, the self that not familiar to you.

---

188. The female who most needs to be uplifted is the female that lies within every male. For the feminine aspect of a man's psyche is a personified portion of the Goddess.

(Inspired By: Arsenothelys)

**If men could better relate to their inner goddesses, I'm sure they would treat women better.

---

189. Just because a beautiful concept or a chthonic theory is one that doesn't spark your interest, or identify with your wisdom, does not prove that concept or theory to be wrong or unreliable.

(Inspired By: Magick)

**Always keep an open mind when experiencing life. The more you learn, the quicker you realize that we are all seeking the divine, we are just taking different paths. Some may take shortcuts to get to that divine experience.

190. I am part of the self-aware consciousness of a sacred living universe, seeking to explore and celebrate itself.

(Inspired By: Self)

**Did that go over your head? Tapping into your universal self, brings no end to your personal creativity.*

---

191. Always allow yourself to feel moments of beauty, ecstatic energy and enraptured joy. For Dionysus is imminent in flesh and in nature, which means you should allow your way of living to deepen your connection to flesh and nature.

(Inspired By: Satyrs)

**Go hug a tree and be proud that we are Dionysus' mysterious initiates, all acts of love and pleasure are his dramatic arts.

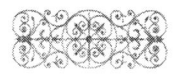

---

192. You can never understand a person's motives, principles, or their decisions, unless you know their past and where they have been.

(Inspired By: Aleister Crowley)

***I've been to many Pagan and Wiccan gatherings, majority of the time when Aleister Crowley's name was brought up it was in a negative light. So, this drove me to read up on him for myself. I did at least a year of study on him for he is a very complex guy, but in no way did I sense a negative vibe, just a man trying to freely find himself in his own unique way.*

---

193. The beauty of Dionysus isn't something you should believe in, but rather something you should experience and enjoy.

(Inspired By: Ampelos)

**Belief implies doubt, knowing is experiencing. I don't believe Dionysus is beautiful, I know He is through experience. I don't believe the pleasures of Dionysus are best, I know they are through touch and flesh.

---

194. Dreams, without actions to obtain them, will forever remain a figment of your imagination.

(Inspired By: My Dream Journal)

**I remember within a dream I had, I asked the Goddess, "Allow society to overlook me, for if they see me, I fear they wouldn't understand."

She replied with a heart-shattering smile, "I understand you."

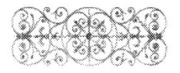

---

195. Courage is a humorous virtue, because it has to be frightened into a person.

(Inspired by: Courage The Cowardly Dog)

**I was once scared to take Acid. It wasn't the drug that I feared, it was me I feared, because Acid opens the mind, and what lies within. And you can only imagine what lies within me. I'm chaos in flesh form, but what pushed me to do it was my fear in letting Dionysus down, for He is the Lord of All Intoxication. So, now you see the humor of courage... Lol

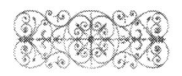

---

196. People can choose a life of adventure with beautiful risks, or they can choose a life of one fucked-up thing after another. Refuse the first, and you get the second.

(Inspired By: Risk)

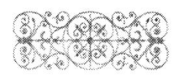

---

197. The Dionysian Nature is a philosophy of life, a spiritual mold of living light and darkness, day and night,

Sun and Moon, Earth and cosmos, life and death, ebb and flow, of joy and of sadness.

(Inspired By: Nietzsche)

***The beautiful thing about it is that you have the freedom to find your own balance within that philosophy.*

---

198. The true spirit of Dionysus comes from the pleasurable hearts and desires of his people. Not from any book of law.

(Inspired By: The Charge of Dionysus)

***The charge of Dionysus is featured at the end of this book.*

---

199. Life's dark moments can create a beautiful light of a person.

(Inspired By: High Max)

***However, this is dependent upon the way a person reacts to these dark moments.*

200. Dionysus always knows the heart. The language of rites you use isn't as important as your intentions.

(Inspired By: My Instincts)

**Blessed are those who are pure (raw) at heart.*

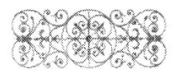

---

201. Our hardships define the personality our character assumes.

(Inspired By: Quote 199)

**Come on, you know you laughed at this. This is some real shit right here.*

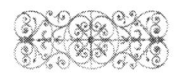

---

202. Nature is meant to be inspirational, as well as Pagan idols.

(Inspired By: Venus of Laussel)

**When I see idols of the gods, they remind me that there's a god within me, inspiring me to see the Divine in human form. For even the Biblical god says humanity is made in the image of Him. Pagan idols remind me of this truth.*

203. How could one path of such central dogmatic authority lead to so great a mystery?

(Inspired By Monotheism)

**A question for those dogmatic religions.*

---

204. People are quick to construct fables to avoid looking reality in the face.

(Inspired By: Ramses II)

**And those who construct these fables attempt to escape reality by misleading others with their twisted stories.*

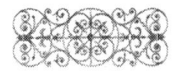

---

205. It is our character that speaks in our favor of our moral excellence.

(Inspired By: My Agathos Daemon)

**They are the guardians of our principles and wisdom.*

206 There is only one way we can heal the pain and suffering of this world. This only requires for us to first heal our own pain and suffering, so that we will no longer unconsciously inflict pain and suffering unto others.

(Inspired By: The Rebirth of Dionysus)

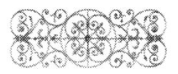

207. Life blossoms on Earth in many different ways. So, strength through diversity mirrors Mother Nature directly.

(Inspired By: Triple fold Diana)

**Why not think that reincarnation also works in more than one way?*

208. Learning how to experience the pleasures of life that's in relation to the goddess' inner guidance, prepares us to drink the nectar of Dionysus without having it drown us.

(Inspired By: Soma)

**The goddess is the one who cured Dionysus of His Madness, so Her inner guidance is helpful.*

209. The journey of life is strenuous, filled with harm and incitement, and there may be a few you may lose before your aim in life is reached.

(Inspired By: Burnt Offerings)

**Just be open to what life brings you.*

210. When the essence of Dionysus does not embody your lovemaking, then there is no true pleasure.

(Inspired By: Dionysian pleasure)

** *"Yes that is both diverse and ecstatic, but is it Dionysian?" This was a question posed to me by my girl during sex.*

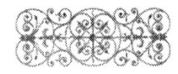

211. Dionysus is not a being that acts, but is the embodiment of the action in itself. He does not save by intervening, but by being. His existence allows us to give birth to our new selves once we kill off what no longer empowers us in our journey.

(Inspired By: Way of the Satyr")

**Dionysus didn't save my life, he made my life worth saving.*

212. When Mother Nature is at Her best, humanity is at its worst.

(Inspired By: Dakota White)

**This is because humanity refuses to be one with Mother Nature. When we learn to live with Her, not against Her, then we can become one with Her beauty instead of making Her seem a horror.*

213. Unshared pleasure, is like an unfinished Dionysian sculpture.

(Inspired By: The Bust of Dionysus)

214. Just as there must be rain with the sun to make all things grow, so must we suffer pain with our joy to experience our positive growth.

(Inspired By: Polygethes)

**Even mistakes and hardships have their place.*

215. Within every experience of Dionysus, one receives far more than he or she seeks.

(Inspired By: Ploutodotes)

** I once went into the woodlands only to give Dionysus an offering. However, after many gulps of wine I ended up dancing to the sound of Nature. Barefoot with the Earth energizing my every step and not at first realizing I had an audience. An owl watched my every move.

I smiled to myself, knowing that Athene made an appearance to my rite which only was supposed to be a burnt offering to Dionysus.

When Dionysus was torn apart by the Titans, it was Athens who preserved His heart (our Phallos), so that He could be reborn.

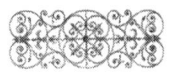

216. True love is not limited, however, people's ideas about love are. The goddess' love permeates and pervades the entire universe. All other forms of love are but expressions, or a reflection of her that exists in the hearts of all.

(Inspired By: Tiamet)

**She welcomes all to affairs with her.

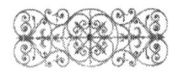

217. STREET JEWEL: The very effort that is put into saving the hood is almost always just a falsified face of the efforts to control it.

(Inspired By: Supreme)

**Watch your hood leaders closely.

218. Nobody ever promised that life would be a rose garden and if you think someone did, just remember that roses also have thorns.

(Inspired By: Gram's rose Garden)

** If hardships and mistakes didn't come along our path, then where would the joy be in overcoming defeat?

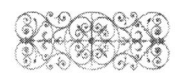

219. The opinion of others, if taken too seriously, can discourage you. Especially if you are unwise, which conforms you to react to situations the way they do. Even if their opinions are false or harmful.

(Inspired By: My Opinion)

**Another person's opinion of you actually says more about that person than it says about you.

220. Dionysian magick is not just something you do or make. It is something the universe does with you once you have awakened to its divinity and sacredness.

(Inspired By: Magnus Bane)

221. Life's motives and meaning are not to be found in some perfectly distant heaven, but discovered along the earthly journey where the blessing, pleasure, wisdom and divinity are ever present.

(Inspired By: Gaia)

**Stop seeking salvation and seek earth.*

---

222. The embodiment of Dionysian pleasure is like a beautiful ivy leaf. Inhale it deeply and share it with those you love.

(Inspired By: The Ivy Crown)

**My proverb.*

---

223. We long for the gods because portions of them lie within us all. We are just longing for what is already a part of us.

(Inspired By: Ancient Mythology)

**This is why the myths of the gods resonate with our own experiences of personal growth, desires and wisdom.*

224. STREET JEWEL: Never kill your adversary when he is already on the verge of hanging himself.

(Inspired By: Tarot Hangman)

*There is no need to attack, because his own twisted ways will be the death of him.

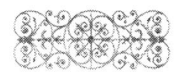

---

225. Challenges should not be feared at all. Opportunities that arise from them should be grasped and utilized to its natural limit.

(Inspired By: Jumanji)

*Life is a contact sport. True understanding is only gained through experience.

---

226. An experience that does not take into account the nature of the living being in its entirety is an illusion. The body is the foundation or instrument of all realizaton.

(Inspired By: Song, "Earth My Body")

*It will be amazing if human beings were awesome at being human beings. (Creatures of the Earth)

227. The journey I chose may be graced with sweet darkness, yet the hearth within burns just bright enough that I may bring life and warmth to those I find along my journey.

(Inspired By: Aries)

**FYI: I'm Leo sun, Aries moon, and Libra Rising.(which also connects me to Dionysus the Liberator (Eleutherios)

228. All the beauty and joy on earth is manifested by the means of an erotic burst of internal energy. Roses release their pollen to the wind and insects. For the creation of Earth is a pleasurable erotic act, an essence of love. Everything that exists embodies this sign and message.

(Inspired By: Yoni)

**The climax of a Dionysian pagan life is not pure ritual. It is a seeking of joy and pleasure and the self-realization of the body. Wine with other safe intoxicating drinks are a part of this joy of living.

229. Mother Nature teaches us that when something stops growing, it begins to die. Metaphorically, we die within once we cease to learn and grow from life experiences.

(Inspired By: The Green Man)

*The Green Man is also another form of Dionysus.

230. Have much gratitude for life, because it gives you a chance to at least experience beauty, pleasure, family and love. Is that not worth being thankful for?

(Inspired By: Charidotes)

Poetic Inspiration

(Raging Iambics)

** Relating to <u>Iambe</u>, a Greek minor goddess of verse, especially scurrilous, ribald humor. In ancient Greece <u>iambus</u> was mainly satirical poetry, lampoons, which did not automatically imply a particular metrical type. Iambic meter took its name from being characteristic of iambi, not vice versa.

"Dear Dionysus"

I stand before you in darkness of truth to acknowledge your worth,
embracing your madness in all forms. Through this existence, I'm glad to serve.
All things signify the beauty that you represent, which I respect.
Though any image may soon perish, but in your love it shall resurrect,
Thoughts of the sunlight that brightens each day,
is the reflection of the masks that display on your face.
Even the moonlight that glows at night,
explains your astonishing dark side that coats that light.
With a love building peace that nourishes life's surface,
confronting humanity's misdeeds which serve your purpose.
A purpose of ecstasy, beauty and sacredness in the powers that be,
and the reincarnation of Dionysus within nature that will put us at ease,
None could explain your truth without proof,
but through Earthly growth is the only root confirming its truth.
The laws of the land describe the merits of your being,

and with every experience we survive, makes your sight worth seeing.
You have given me life and in this representation, I must pollute mankind,
with the essence of your bliss that will illuminate visions of the blind.
Such sacrifices have paved the way for your children to live eternally in paradise,
where we shall forever chant your worth during the evolution of the afterlife...

Bios Dionusou

**When i first wrote this poem I gave it to Dionysus as a burnt offering. As the smoke blew within natures wind, He heard every word. So now I give it to my Dionysian pagans as a written offering. He approves.

"Liber Dionysus"

(Idolotry)

It feels like my lifeline is seduced into a trance,
while worshipping your figure polished in the highlights of your stance.
As I make a grandstand, there is this pressure throbbing in my head,
As if I'm juggling with my thoughts where the frenzy seems to dance.

(So I bow before you)

An artistical work of liberal stone art you are,
sure that the framework of your wild side was much harder to carve,
but on any given Anthesteria, your idol beauty bringeth smiles that twinkle like stars.
The same delicate beauty that brings madness to an ever so beating heart.

(I light the candles)

This is not a love story of Beauty and the Beast,
it's more like a suitable attraction with features of you and me.
Envisioning a chaotic future with us as one beautiful piece,

the symbol of enraptured love connected by a force that refuses to ease.

(I burn the incense)

The very sight of you is enticing in many ways,
an astonishing exhibit that glosses under any shade.
A shrine of its own no one can duplicate nor imitate,
The art of your creation has relations to night and day...

(I sip the wine)

Bios Dionusou

** *This poem was inspired by how jealous my ex-girl was over the bond I had with my Dionysus idol. She became so mad one day, she told all of her friends that I was a stupid idol worshipper. The mistake she made was even trying to compare herself to Dionysus.*

"The Beauty of Ariadne"

(My handfasted mate)

The quality of being very pleasing,
as in form wild and free, are astonishingly intriguing,
defining its meaning, so you will recognize
that if a blindfold was placed over the world, you'd stand out as heaven's eyes.
Having dignifying richness and purifying taste
with an attitude filled with a blissful passion and glorifying grace
using this opportunity to handfast you
as being the queen that only a king can relate to.
Your beauty is gorgeous in every aspect,
so deep and enormous that none can grasp that
though I am willing to see how far this passion can go or flow.
Living freely is the only rule in paradise,
the place where we will reunite in the afterlife.
With LOVE being the key, we must keep.
Where "Dionysian Rites" is the street we'll take to succeed.
As we exchange and hunt each other,
forever we shall reap the labor of the natural wild beauty of one another.

Bios Dionusou

"The Gods In You"

(Dionysus Arsenothelys)

To define the Yang to Yin's feminism,
is retracted through qualities regarded as characteristics as a god's mannerism.
Designated from the terminology of masculinity,
but essential to embracing its birth side of maternity.
This combination consists of its own willing gestures,
which couldn't be prevented by any effective measures.
Though these qualities make your natural being versatile in a variety of ways,
displaying great atypical strengths of moral might that any trait can relate.
This is a description of why your inner being is so divine in the gods' grace.
Under this guideline of divinity comes inspirational EMINENCE,
that is often seen manifested within distinctive charisma
To care, to provide, to protect your domain.
Through sweat and pain, yet you don't complain,
because there is a godly goddess within you that knows no shame.

So, to my maenads and nymphs, I would like
   to dedicate to you,
this testament of sacred truth, for you must
   adopt to
every particle of the gods in you...

      Bios Dionusou

"This is my Home"

(Here with you)

Describe a place that defines where we lay,
without shades that hide another truth that we aim to penetrate.
No place is as great as this Dionysiac faith.
In a state of grace we strive to evade
the chaotic side of nature that thrives off of the Fates.
Through love and beauty our eyes see all things sacred.
I can't think of losing this feeling,
because there's sincerely so many masks embodied in this feeling.
I never knew of its healing, its Dionysian revealing.
I smile deeply while thinking of the joy of simply being here.
Like the eyes of the blind whose vision is seeing fear.
This sensation is just another mystery of not seeing clear.
I would be less without this knowledge,
but all blessed be to recognize its power.
Nothing could devour the blossoming of wisdom's unique flower.
Who are you? Everything.
An energy that takes me places I have never been.

Beyond the highest of heights on a flight that I'll never land.
The beginning is now behind us,
and the destination ends once we find love.
From one soul to Gaia, its divine love, our love...

Bios Dionusou

**Since birth I have always felt that Earth was my home. So they can have their salvation of some distant heaven. I am honored to call Earth my paradise. Gaia lives!

"Kissed By The Ivy"

(Kissos)

I have grown to love you unconditionally,
through this affair of loving you that has blossomed tremendously.
In crossing your path you've become an ecstatic religion.
Discovering the truth of me being a Satyr and the truth of loving a pleasurable spirit.
Your identity is a particle of the origin that defines how the whole of life caresses me,
because I have embraced your heart, I'm now living eternally, peacefully.
You are everything, because everything is beautiful.
You should know that all of what you possess aligns everywhere along the universe.
What does it mean to feel this side of loving you?
When any object that opposes you becomes a material disvalue as heavens proof.
Which is why I am thankful for the blessing of your presence,
This exchange of us is of another essence.
To share with you these words, they are modest and humble.
Sincerely, yours truly... Your Dionysian lover...

Bios Dionusou

"To Inhale a Maenad"

(Denise)

With each kiss our energy pollinates the world with what the heart releases, when it feels the most.
Shall we propose a Dionysian toast?
To the wonderful creation of a love that we have grown to know
Understanding each other like birds whose wings are used to huddle rather than fly,
shielding you from life's danger that drips from a patriarchal sky.
My life is your life and your flesh is my love,
two intertwined bodies makes the tension rise above.
Aroused from what is displayed in your pupils,
with each lick that makes you shake in ways that you are not used to.
Our hearts illuminate the day, give me a kiss.
Where we see each other in its radiance,
what a beautiful sensation of the way that we are made of this.

Bios Dionusou

"My Agathos Daemon"

(Two in One)

Settling for less says that you're less than what you have settled for.
Perhaps this is just another metaphor—nothing less or more standing before Hel's door.
Wishing for the most beautiful chthonic daemon, one that I've yet met before,
my better core chanting that I am forever yours,
through thick and thin and weathered storms.
All blessed be to know that you are my counterpart bringing out the best in me,
a reflection of what's left in me.
Can't you see that it's your air I breathe, your sows I reap, your eyes from those I see?
You are another sight of me and your heart is where I sleep.
Through those masked pupils seeing no difference in the figure that looks back at me,
a picture given in vivid description duplicated through relations.
Two of a kind like the eyes on our faces,
we vibe off patience not through hatred,
nor manipulated in other areas of communication.

We originated one of the greatest superlative combinations,
spoken silently in muted truth, one image.
Two hearts in competition, with no finish,
under one condition that this is done,
through the creation of the universe that considers us one...

Bios Dionusou

*When I speak of Hel, I'm speaking on the Goddess Hel, whose realm is of rebirth, not torturous like the patriarchal hell. All hail the Queen of Hel!

"My Cleopatra"

(My distant Ancestor)

Always and forever, describes you and me.
Two hearts conjoined into one soul,
two lives, but our love is one whole.
Captivated by the gods that pointed me in your direction,
touched by what has by far been the greatest blessing of all essence.
One stroke, two strokes, three strokes,
chasing pleasures that spell words that only we know.
It's pure ecstasy when you are next to me,
and our encounters are testaments that define our destiny.
No shame in the mentioning of your name,
but I certainly make your name my final claim.
With this being the future that we will represent,
there's no neglecting it, forever within your queenship,
our love will never end...

Bios Dionusou

"Dramatic Parables"

(Uncomparable)

So much depends on the drumming of the soul that opens to hear
the quieting of the mind that banishes the fear..
The acceptance of others that softens the truth,
and the truth is that you are incomparable to any other, no kingship is the same as you.
You're distinctively of eminence,
have I not considered your existence for any significance?
Then I would not contribute the sentiment that's solidified
the connection that we made dearer than other elements of Immanence.
To compare any two things is a clear indication that those two things are unrelated.
Therefore they are incomparable, because both have their own values to the object that unified their relation.
My love for you outlasted my notions of love.
From us I found the meaning of life through our sacred blood.
If you understand my frenzy for you, then you would know that this feeling is of another nature.

It's beyond anything major, more like the Maker.
Reversing your Inquiry is just a form of reciprocation,
when placed in a similar situation then you wouldn't be able to understand a parable that cannot be invaded...

Bios Dionusou

"Twin Suns"

An entity without material reality (my Persephone),
is something we must cherish with intensified love.
Admired ritually and indefinitely,
the intensity of a spirit lies within its own measurements.
In the body of a soul where life's principles are inherited.
When the moral and emotional part of us is shared with another,
it is then regarded as an essential substance where they are no longer considered a couple.
More like a completed whole of two people combining spiritual forces with each other.
Exchanging vital warmth in a higher quality of magic as two lovers.
A twin sun is the identical portion of another individual,
not considered two separate individuals, but as one organism.
Solemnly, their intertwined emotions are unapproachable.
They embody the gods which is so damn noticeable.
Descriptions of one another in each other's dreams of what reality holds,

instigating similar affection through the sight of what their galaxy shows.
Behold of what is commonly known,
in a complexion that has established itself as being timely consoled,
to recognize themselves as twin suns.
It's defined when two souls are related in every natural way,
when every aspect beyond a living nation,
mind, body, heart and spirit, shall they connect in any creation...

Bios Dionusou

***We are the same Nocturnal Sun, Dionysus and me. I am the light that radiates from that sun and He is the warmth that is felt from that sun.*

"The Essence of Dionysus"

(Free Love)

Seeking a desire that most of us have never seen,
though its silhouette became a vision in a wet dream.
It shines in darkness as it glows in day,
signifying beauty and pleasure in a most conspicuous way.
Its demand for freedom and ecstasy is a beautiful ascent,
boundless is its allegiance to anyone who accepts,
Blessed deliverance within its limits.
Once you have set out to capture this essence within your grip,
remember that it will only please those who treat it well
and to whom are true to self so never let it slip.
The unconscious fear of desire for one will imprison its spirit,
shielding it from being true to its one great love, of freedom to experiment.
This type of central exchange should be free to the whole of humanity,
freedom to pursue it is rather sacred - it's a beautiful profanity...

Bios Dionusou

"Heresy"

(Pen of a Heretic)

My knowledge is matter of fact, to attack the myth of Christianity.

Abstract from their overreacted jealous made god.

Who is known to subtract the beauty with a counteract to distract our duty.

A contract to impact a pack with a twisted divine tact is nothing but a falsely act.

Divinity comes from within, that's a known fact. Christianity is not the origins of humanity, just do your history.

More like the origins of insanity, disrespecting the goddess with the worst profanity.

It's no mystery, I foresaw the evil of Constantine, the lies of Augustine, the truth about Mary Magdalene.

Between this complex war machine, I resurrect with every full thirteen with the same routine to acknowledge my goddess.

Their obedience is an offense to justify their malevolence with the intent to influence no intelligence.

History is evidence against this self-defense religious reference,

showing that their residence and suspenseful teaching is common war sense.

Nothing holy, just abandonment from the divine, with ill contempt and lies.
Then asking you to repent from the evil you underwent with torment.
Yet my element is nourishment to the body, excellent for the mind, irrelevant to their lies.
I am Karneious Theones living a Dionysian type of life.

Bios Dionusou

**This is my earliest stage of poetry, my teenage years when I felt some type of way about how Christianity treated us pagans.

Growing up I had to switch my style of poetic wordplay (switch my masks) I had to stop being judgmental.

Now I allow the Muses to guide my hand. However being that this is a poetic journal of my experiences, I must editorially include my earliest stages of poetic anger. Don't judge me so harshly, I was young and very emotional.

Here's three more of my earliest style poems... though I no longer write in this style.

"So Pagan"

(Io Euoi)

Drink of me and intoxicate the mind with dandelion Wine, allowing my richness and ecstasy of life to generate your kind,
it's great to circulate the Phallic Pole, celebrate to graduate your old soul, communicating with the gods to fertilize the
harvest, educated by the forest, never hesitate to participate the hardest, please meditate to gravitate the holistic universe,
rotate the elements to activate the floodgate in the West to medicate this world with the blessings of the Graces, my birthdate
will procreate to populate with the Fates, then I shall terminate the outdate of the Christian debate, when I'm gone cremate this
shell to allow my flesh to duplicate this world, chanting to separate my Darkself from self-hate as the world simulate to a solid
state, hold up 'wait', how could they violate then put god's name on it to translate their false ways to suffocate the ones who
originated their Faith? This is a first-rate double case of hate to depopulate the states, how could y'all cooperate with fakes?
Who assassinated our Mates (goddesses)?

Bios Dionusou

"Thriambos"

(Anax)

Blessed are the frenzy at heart,
With permission to position the Dionysian state of Art,
Mission of Living is to give healthy nutrition to our old religion,
Divine ambition is our definition to edition the Satyr's commission,
Names of Power: Gillian, Artemis, Dionysus, and Pan,
Isle of Man, Blessed Be In Peace Marianne my herstorian,
Please pentagram my diagram of life,
Campaign my original rites,
Seriously, reincarnate my elders for their beliefs were a notorious sight,
The Way Of The Satyr, a rebirth of their Nocturnal Light...

Bios Dionusou

"Parnassian"

My atmosphere is dear to cheer the Great Diana and Her fellow deer.

My home is protected by the chaotic powers of my Dionysian Purple Chandelier,

To engineer my hemisphere making it clear to hear my deity peers,

The Satyr's souvenir is sincere-blessing myself as a volunteer to pioneer our career,

Hidden mystery within my poetry to uncover the success,

Undress the unblessed with our colorless soul, Caress the joyfulness,

Suppress the stress, Embrace the flesh, Welcome to my craftiness.

Yes we are weaponless-obsessed with ancestress,

but nevertheless my ladies headdress is never flowerless,

Our consciousness is the beauty of right mindedness, More or less self-righteousness.

Chanting to the far east allowing the high Priest to bless the Harvest feast,

Peace and Love, so mote it be.

Its Ptolemaic history a lot of mystery absolute bloodroot for our love,

My attribute (Karneios) will uproot the forbidden fruit from the mud,

To prosecute the lies, Execute their adopted myths, then substitute their pollute
to salute the goddess passionate fruit for our lives,
Singing beautiful words while implanting magickal herbs,
My visionary is necessary, Io Euoi Io Euoi to my solitaries,
Either way we are legendary, Contrary to Rosemary,
Slowly take a breath now my revolutionary means every one of your patriarchal religions
is hereditary to OUR evolutionary beliefs, do your history...

Bios Dionusou

**This was the last poem I wrote as a teen in trying to make everything rhyme. Some of my Pagan friends love my new style of poetry and others love my old earlier style.

As for me I just follow my intuition and surrender to the Muses as They sing through my poetry, esp. Euterpe and the Satyr TITYROI (Tityri) who is a Flute-playing Satyr in the train of the god Dionysus.

"Forever He Who Causes Me To Stumble"

(Sphaleotas)

Sphaleotas, You & I for ages long,
Frenzied together with hidden song,
Worshipped the Mask, a god who frees,
No sensation unexplored, a dramatic tease,
Perhaps we Panicked 'til dawn did break,
Causing all the Satyrs on Nysa to wake,
Wrestling with Dragons a secret of kind,
Twin Flames discovered within our mysterious sign,
Io Euoi Io Euoi, dripping from our lips like nectar,
Serpentine Pleasures, get better and better,
While hiding behind our fiction which reveals our truth,
Dionysus Liberates Within aspects of You...
I Love You

Bios Dionusou

"Dramatic Birth"

(Karneios)

When madness abounds what do I do?
Beloved Dark Dionysus I turn to you,
For amongst the frenzy it's easy to discover,
A Masked aspect of you acting undercover,
Because it's Fated that we engage in this dance,
Freedom is our gift and this is my chance,
Ariadne, Aphrodite, Athens and Artemis,
Demeter, Gaea and all others I've not forgot,
Dionysian Ladies who aid in the shedding of skin,
The cycle demands death in order to begin,
Pass the chaos of frustration if I stop and listen,
I will hear You there with words of wisdom,
Telling me, "Stop running from the skin that clings to your flesh,
the process of shedding is only a test,
just like a child in the womb the birth can be frightening,
but if you let me dark satyr, I'll be there with open arms, inviting
you to New Love, New Senses, New Life and New Truth,
trust Me and just continue to push through,
know this though the birth is only as hard as you make it,

you've shedded much skin in the past, you know you can take this,
so instead of making it hard and painful,
relax, laugh, dance and let your birth be aimful,
I love you horn son, but as you well know the choice is yours,
just know I am here with love and madness to pour forth."
And with that the noise subsides and wine begins to flow,
I will trust You Dark Dionysus and finally let go...

Bios Dionusou

"Inner Nysa"

(Mt.Nysa)

As I descend into the depths of my own darkness,
Who I am is revealed in greater starkness,
The faces of me I've shoved down and suppressed,
In truth calls forth the best of my best,
No longer chasing ascension, resting in my descension,
Right or wrong no longer exist within my universal perception,
My underworld has become my sweet wonderland,
of exploration, discovery and transformation, my heartland...

Bios Dionusou

**Mt. Nysa—a divine, mythic mountain where Dionysus was raised by Nymphs, Maenads and Satyrs. However, within The Way Of The Satyr, we say that Mt. Nysa truly lies within each initiate. This is why there were so many claims to where Mt. Nysa originated. It depended on the initiate... yet some claims say that Mt. Nysa was originated in Italy... Another connection to me.

"The Divine Child"

(Lil john john)

He emerged from the essence of Earth
    A thousand moons ago,
Embodying Himself throughout all Nature
    His ways are to ebb and flow,
I completely opened my heart to Him
    though I didn't know my place,
He swiftly devoured my core
    and I suddenly became aware of His ways,
Within the very realm of darkness
    He taught me the pulse of life,
"In order for things to truly live
    death must replace all life,
never fear the Nature of Me
    for I am the essence of you,
rebirth will follow the process
    once you remember your own truth."
The burst of light was radiant
    and then I felt the embrace,
Sensing the rhythm of my mother's heart
    as I gazed up upon her face,
she smiled and named me Karneios Theones
    and then she fed me her nipple,
Life anew, death in due
    it is truly beyond the mental...

    Bios Dionusou

"I Invoke Thee"

(Arsenothelys)

Goddess of the Light and God of shadows
witness and blessed my spiritual battles
    within and without
In the face of chaotic pleasure where there is no doubt
Do I understand? Just about
Yet understanding is not my key
I have perfect trust when experiencing 'SHE'
    A Divine Reality
No Amen but Blessed Be
Who needs confessions when there's complete trust
Who needs suppression when there's Divine Lust
When there is life there also must be Dust
Wise and honorable Maenad Raging One of All
I rejoice in what is Short and what is Tall
What is Risen and what eventually must Fall
I drift with frenzy in the Arts of the Dramatic
That all things are as they should be
Love and Madness is what it should be
From the West Forest of the deep seas
    I Invoke Thee I Invoke Thee
Forms the eternal passions of your Union
Balance me Balance Thee
    All Blessed Be...

Bios Dionusou

"Ivy Crown"

How could I not speak these words of dignity,
When your Frenzy is the meaning of my history,
From the outside looking in we are seen as a Mystery,
My ability to speak poetry with our Royalty unites US eternally,
Gazing into your eyes is the remedy to my injury,
Your heartbeat plays a melody that dictates my legacy,
I scream out Io Euoi because in the presence of your sincerity,
I apparently become enchanted by your reality,
Could this be poetry or just a prophecy of our totality,
Within the celebration of Anthesteria you are my Ivy Queen,
The Great Rite on every full thirteen, my Ecstatic dream,
Have you not seen the unseen-purified the unclean?
I must confess, but nevertheless though
Without You in my life I am pleasureless,
I'm obsess... Yes... Possessed with your Quest,
Impressed with your ability to leave me motionless,
It Can't be denied how Your love has multiplied the meaning of my life,
Chant me to Sleep, Sweet Bacchus, sing me a lullaby,

Glorify our purpose which dignifies Our Worship,
Allow my tongue to testify its desire across your essence,
To signify that there's pretty much more blessings,
Dare call Our lust sin and even the Rabbi has the right to die,
I'm just joking, We only know Passion and Love,
Now toast to the gods, have a drink of Our Blood,
The Life force... of Course...

Bios Dionusou

**Please don't take my jokes so harshly. They are very much inspired by the goddess Iambe and Dionysus's Son Priapos, where licentious jokes have their place.

"Chaotic Thoughts"

Twisted... Absurd, ill-advised logic,
Inflamed shadows, provoking forsaken topics,
Gnostic... No!!! Toxic... Yes!!! In every way possible,
Kiss of insanity and foreplay not logical,
Obstacles... Many!!! Which only brings more confusion,
I don't want to gain reason, is this faith or illusion,
In finding truth... do I pursue it or lose it?
Allusions... Allusions... What the fuck am I pursuing,
Darkness it seems is the only thing rooting,
Fertilizing my flesh... Forbidden seeds are intruding...

Bios Dionusou

"A Touch Of Madness"

The pressure comes from left to right,
Demanding and pushing to do as they like,
Faces, Voices, Whispers and Screams,
Laughing, Smiling, Kind and mean,
So many, So loud , I can't see straight,
Clarity eludes me, don't let it be too late,
Overwhelming, all consuming, insanity,
Questioning is this really what it takes to be set free,
To lose all sense of self and surrendering to the abyss,
Beloved Lord Dionysus who enchants with a kiss,
The void, the darkness, the chaos and fight,
Only to realize in the depths of the night,
The Daemon, The Horned One, the 'So-called' enemy,
Is but a familiar Mask staring right back at me,
Own it, face it, know this is part of self,
Only then can I return and create myself,
Suddenly a flicker, the tiniest of light,
Gives hope and illumination to this current plight,
Follow and with new wisdom come back to life,
Knowing now how to handle the difficult price,
Learn from, transform and shed the remainder of skin,
So as you dance with the abyss the Lady will give birth again,
To new visions, new hope, all it took was letting go
of my own worst enemy, my very own ego...

Bios Dionusou

"A Licentiousness Mystery"

(Cuckoldry)

At times I question myself that whether or not this Love shit really matters,
The more I stare at you I find myself enveloped inside your heart rather
thinking there's a better place for me to start,
Only then that I realize what truly matters in our place,
Because it has taken a multitude of losses for us to reach this phase,
Losses that never would've counted for anything, useless art,
But when I found a comfortable place in your heart,
I was touched by something hard that only Love can open the senses of,
In a way that made me see and embrace my own truth, you're my witness, luv,
It's funny how we can bring about the sacredness in things and situations from the tools we're given,
and in this case my tool is you, perfidious mission not to mention,
You've opened something within me that I thought didn't exist,
And you did it all by accepting me into your Yoni, taking a Nocturnal Risk,
And I just want to say the opposite of Thank You... You Beautiful Witch...

Bios Dionusou

"ANANCE (Thee) Necessity"

(Another Daemon)

Finding Dark arms once again,
Darkness so dark I can't see a thing,
Feeling the start of a deep soul scream,
Breath getting short as the buildup begins,
Fear gaining strength wanting to befriend,
We've danced before but never this intense,
Coming forth from within a most intimate kiss,
Unable to see and nowhere to flee,
I realize this dance is about the Daemon deepest in me,
My Satyr of true Darkness and loss of control,
Anance whispers, "Become the ebb that truly flows."
Muscle by muscle I feel the tension release,
Finally my lungs are able to breathe,
Love wraps around me and my soul flies and soars,
As Darkness speaks to my heart, "There is so much more
when you dance with me in perfect frenzy and Love.
You will experience things you can't even dream of.
Come with me Karneios and rest in my arms,
Allow your Dark Daemon the care of your heart…"

Bios Dionusou

"First Sight"

Silently you observed like a temple statue,
As I twisted, twirled and threw grapes at you,
Until I was breathless, reckless and intoxicated,
With the Mad movement of my own body, consecrated.
Yet, in that very instant I knew all was lost,
As for Dionysus, all was gained at a beautiful cost,
And the swelling of unconditional love filled my mind,
The vines whispered to me as the Wine filled my Shrine,
Call it god, call it Fate or my own intuition,
You can say its unwise, foolish or downright fiction,
But you can't deny that my life has come to a frenzy addiction,
The universe takes care of those who don't fight with patience,
I'm chaotic fire I go wherever the wind takes me,
And let Fate take my hand in whoever embraces me faithfully,
Truly within this moment I feel myself immense,
Kin to the fiery stars, fucking in the Greek Love of men,
Knowing myself free and flowing-bound by no law,
I am the vine. You are the branches found by my paw,

Wine pulsating through my veins at the sight of your presence,
She who wears the Ivy Crown should be honored and blessed...

        Bios Dionusou

"My Dionysian Eye"

People say they want spoken word
yet don't understand what's spoken,
    They claim its broken
I laugh! Why? Because their mind is stolen
    No joking
However, my sense of humor is potent,
My sense of desire is Poking,
I laugh! No for real what I speak creates life,
When I Dance you die-When I laugh you cry,
    I'm Mystery
    Try understanding the Eye, I...

        Bios Dionusou

"I Am, Who I Am"

I'm the heat of a lion's breath
I'm the hallucination to a person on meth
I'm the sharpness of a Daemon's horn
I'm that moment when Wine is born
I'm one of a kind, To all mankind
I'm the Darkness that Light can't find
I'm the depths of the deepest cave
I'm that very poison that you crave
I'm the lost as well as the found
I'm my Father's Ivy Crown
I'm the Satyr in the church's pew
I'm the portal to walk through
I'm a Nymph's smile during a Summer breeze
I'm the Honeycomb of a thousand Bees
I'm the last of a Horn'd breed
I'm a million planted seeds
I'm the center of every place
I'm the nationality of every race
I'm the outcome of an unanswered prayer
I'm the courage that banishes fear
I'm pleasure after a long day of pain
I'm a concept that can't be tamed
The very Truth that can't be claimed...

Bios Dionusou

**My Therapist asked me to write her a poem that was based on Identity, asking me who I thought I was.

My immediate response was I didn't know, because I was still creating myself at the time, but she asked me to look deeply within. And this was the poem I wrote her. You should have seen her reaction when she read it. It was priceless. I basked in her reaction... Lol

"The Way Of The Satyr"

(We Are)

Who are the Initiates of your Path?
We are the Elements that dance upon creation—(Auxites)
We are what's relevant during the process of cremation—(Aigobolos)
We are the wounds of the rawest sacrifice—(Isodaites)
We are the embodiment of what's most sacred in life—(Anax)
We are thoughts that just can't be pondered on—(Teletarches)
We are Death, an abortion of the unborn—(Anthroporaistes)
We show you our Mask then we lift it—(Tauropon)
We are cursed as well as the gifted—(Diphyes)
We are the chants of a thousand Witches—(Iackhos)
We are the inspiration of a thousand wishes—(Polygethes)
We are keepers of the misunderstood—(Manikos)
We are Dionysian Pagans, don't get it misunderstood—(Bios Dionusou)
We are secrets that wish not to be spoken—(Kryphios)
We are pleasures that must be woken—(Orthos)
We are emotions which cannot be ignored—(Luaeus)

We are the forbidden Wine that must be poured—
(Botryophoros)
We are what your ashamed to be—(Arsenothelys)
We are the Darkness that the blind must see—
(Nyktelios)
We are gentle rain that caresses the flesh—(Hues)
We are fangs that penetrate the breast—(Zagreus)
We are the weariness of the unrest—(Sphaleotas)
We are the loneliness of the unblessed—(Arretos)
We are the vision that goes beyond view—
(Mantis)
We are Io Euoi Mystics, the complete opposite of you—(Euios)

Bios Dionusou

**The titles I used at the end of my sentences are Epithets (Aspects) of Dionysus. I will give you a list of their meaning so to give you a glimpse of the mystery of why I chose to use it at the end of the sentence.

Auxites: bringer of growth. Aigobolos: slayer of goats. Isodaites: divider of sacrificial meat.

Anax: lord. Teletarches: lord of initiations. Anthroporraistes: slayer of men. Tauropon: bull-faced.

Diphyes: two-natured. Iackhos: crier, caller. Polygethes: bringer of many joys. Manikos: mad one.

Bios Dionusou: is not actually an Epithet, but a Dionysian saying that means 'Dionysian Life'.

Kryphios: hidden, secret. Orthos: the erect. Luaeus: he who frees.

Botryophoros: bearer of grape clusters.

Arsenothelys: man-womanly. Nyktelios: nocturnal. Hues: of moisture.

Zagreus: hunter-is the first incarnation of Dionysus.

Sphaleotas: he who causes stumbling. Mantis: prophet,seer. Euios: from the ritual cry. Arretos: ineffable.

"Zagreus... son born to Zeus in dragon bed by Persephone, the consort of the black-robed king of the underworld..."

Dionysiaca, 5.562ff, Nonnus c. 500 CE

"Dear Depression"

Do you even care about my life?
Do you think you are helping me?
Because I don't care about life no more
Because of you
Depression, why are you not letting me live my life?
I'm so tired of being there for people and then they push me away
I'm tired of loving people and they don't love me back
I'm tired of living like this
Why are you doing this to me?
But most of all I'm tired of living a lie
I'm tired of when I go home I think about ending it all I'm so done
But you might know that I'm doing this because I want attention
But no, I have been felt like it for such a long time
that is not what you want feel like
I'm tired of crying
Feel like I'm nothing
I have been through a lot in my life
I'm so done
I have to go, this bullshit-ass school that I don't want to be in, because I get talk about every day
People say that I'm fat that my belly
Hangs over my pants
Now I feel death is the one way that I can be happy

I have tried it, but it never works. Why god? I
    don't want to be here no more
I have no one that gets it. I have been trying to cut
    my vein but it never works
So why do I have to go through this?
My arm cover is cut And I can't stop, because that
    is how I feel better
or I think that how you get my madness out... then
    I feel bad
I feel like I'm letting people down because, go
    home and cut myself

I'm about done with life keep saying that and
    when I trying it never work.

But on strike three I'm not gonna to stop til I'm
    dead

Well with that being said
I love you so much
You are my world
Farewell
I will be looking down at you

By: Liyah

**This poem is by my beautiful niece. No, she isn't a Dionysian yet the dark beauty that graces her poem is very Dionysian and I'm sure Dionysus understands her pain. For I ask Him to look over her every night. I love you, Liyah, my beautiful goddess!!!

"Dionysus is Alive"

(The Flip side)

Look around. Tell me, what makes you cry?
For me, it's the beauty of life, just look to the sky.
For every one death, many others are born,
but don't take this for granted or you will be torn.
It tugs at my heart,
His Frenzy awakens.
It comes with a start,
My whole world is shaken.
Wake up today, have so many desires,
Tomorrow, a new Mask, I'll burn them on pyres.
I can't begin to explain how this makes me feel.
Ecstatic drunk to meditating monk,
this sensation is surreal.
Dionysus is alive, I'm here to let you know,
the bushes, the trees
All show His glow.
The birds and the bees, yes, can't you see.
But more than that He is your feelings, just look He resides.
Dionysus is in all things (You), Dionysus is Alive...

By: Dakota 'Slip' White

Bios Dionusou

Thriambos Offerings

(Triumphal Hymns)

**Thriambos is what I like to call Prayers dedicated to Dionysus. For it is an epithet of Dionysus which means Triumphal Hymns. And that's exactly what my prayers are to Him—Triumphal Hymns. However, they are also my burnt offerings.

I tend to write these Prayers down and burn them so to mirror the myth of Dionysus being born out of fire. Dramatic, I know. Yet, Dionysus is the Father of Drama.

When our actions tend to mirror the myth of the gods, they seem to be more effective—at least in my experiences. So, here are Triumphant Hymns (Prayers) that will inspire you to create your own.

I've also featured Prayers from other Pagans who have a place in their heart for Dionysus. We have come together to share how we honor Dionysus through prayer, in thanks for the many ecstatic blessings He has given us in the past and present.

May these Dionysian Hymns be pleasing to Your ears Father.

Io Euoi Io Euoi

Dionusou Anax,

I drink of You today, grateful that You will place the mighty Thyrus in my hands,
gracing me in fawn skin. I crave to dwell in Your presence-wild and untamed.
I want to know Your pleasures in every way They can be known.
Destroy and rebuild me in Your image so that I come to please You better.
Crown me in Your Ivy and choke me with Your vine in ways that I know both pleasure and pain,
for You are the uniter of opposites. I seek the very truth of who You are,
because I know that You embody the very truth of who I am.....

Io Euoi !!!

** *"Yea; I shall place a Thyrus in thy hand. And shall array thee in a dappled fawn skin." – Dionysus*

(Bakchai) 98. James M Pryse

Akratophoros,

Inspire me to set aside time each day to drink with You alone.

As I sacrifice my time before You, bless me to love ecstatically,

becoming the mirror of Your beloved Ampelos. Help me to love more like You,

for if anyone thirsts, let them come drink of You. Because the worlds a dry place without You.

I come to You this day and drink deeply of Your wine.

I know You are Non-attachable yet connected to All.

I also know there's deeper Mysteries within Your presence

that I long to experience. Possess my senses as I crave Your frenzy,

so that I may dwell in Nysa like never before....

Io Euoi !!!

** *"But, She, foaming at the mouth and twisting her eyes all about... was possessed by Bacchus (Dionysus)."*

The Bacchac, 1124-1129

Euripides, c. 400 BCE

Charidotes,

I pray that I ever be in Your graceful favor, O Dionysus giver of grace.
According to Your ecstatic kindness, according to the multitude of Your chaotic blessings,
blot out any conformalities. Create in me a natural wild heart
and renew a free spirit within me.
Do not banish me away from your exuberant epiphany,
and do not take Your Earthly spirit from me.
If there is any judgmental views in me,
devour such ways and lead me in the way of everlasting bliss.
Expose to me the truth of my nature so that I can celebrate it fully.
Excite me to frenzy before Your presence. I want Your madness
so that times of refreshing may come from Your Liberation...

Io Euoi !!!

** *"There was no god more present than Dionysus."*

Vikki Bramshaw (Dionysus: Exciter To Frenzy)

Auxites,

Teach me to embrace, better yet to caress the moments of my life
that are hard to get my arms around.
Enable my senses to see and feel You in those moments.
Help me to always appease the abundance
of Your blessed deliverance towards me.
I surrender to You the darkest parts of myself,
I trust You to open my eyes to see all You have for me in them.
Expose to me the Dionysian fullness of it all.
Thanks to you that I can be filled
with the joy of Your presence in every moment I seek,
because You have given me the hunger I need for whatever comes my way...

Io Euoi !!!

** *"Dionysus...was god of wine, and the god of ecstasy and terror, of wildness and the most blessed deliverance ".*

Jean S Bolen(God is In Everyman)

A Dionysian Prayer,

Great Dionysus, Father of All things ecstatic,
when they ask to see my book of Dionysian
 Prayers,
I show them wonderful cuts drawn
ecstatically of veins on the underside of an Ivy
 leaf,
telling them I believe in the ripened grapes
squashed and drained against bare feet on an
Anthesteria Spring and in Nights so Dark the
starry Heavens expose Herself Madly, pouring
rays of fiery nocturnal light to Earth, and telling
them how I drank the sacred wine of honeysuckle
with beautiful Lenaia and of Her softness in
 which
She taught me that pleasure is Life's reward...

Io Euoi !!!

**Lenaia is a Dionysian festival, however the title Lenaia derives from the name Lenai, which is a chorus of frenzied women worshippers of Dionysus, related to the Baccae and Maenads.

Praying For Madness

May Your Madness ebb through me,
may it bring me Divine ecstacy
May You nurture my flesh & Pleasures,
may it embody Your Mad recipe
May You Dionysus pollute my fears,
may that pollution purify my epiphany
May it soothe my beautiful wounds
may all Your blessings be meant for me
May You work through me,
may I find You with in...

Io Euoi !!!

** *"The madness which is called Dionysus is no sickness, no debility in life,*
but a companion of life at its healthiest.
It is the tumult which erupts from its innermost recesses
when they mature and force their way to the surface.
It is the madness inherent in the womb of the mother."

- Walter F. Otto ' Dionysus(Myth and Cult)

Dionysus,

You are my namesake
and my life's duty is connected to You.
You are everything I have ever been
ecstatically in favor of.
You free me when You use me as a vessel
to carry Your work into the world.
I dedicate my time in this shell
to living in accordance with Your way.

Euoi!

By: Denise Major-Dodge

**Denise I truly appreciate you sharing this Prayer with me because it actually inspired me in many ways.
Through your visions I found solace.
Did I ever thank you for sharing such a gift with me?
It wouldn't hurt to repeat it.
Thanks Maenad for that breakdown of my astrology sign and planets,
how you showed me the many way I am connected to our Lord Dionysus.
Io Euoi Io Euoi..
And for all who don't know, the name Denise derives from the name Dionysus.

Evoe Zagreus,

Source of our deathless spirit.

Evoe Auxitês!
Let our spirits grow with your eternal presence.

Evoe Lyseus, our Liberator,
Guide us out of the ultimate prison,
Free us with your holy blood.

My lips always touching your wine,
I, always in ecstasy with your essence,

Let the thyrsus stay in our hands forever,
And claim us as your thíasos,
To travel with you through eternity..

By: Erdem Kutlu

IAOM, Dionysus!

Husband, Brother, Father! Aye, your Bryde, vow to resurrect You, through love,
which is magick on every dimension of this universe. Our union will construct
the Matri(x) of the New Aeon. The Gods will be filled with joy, envy and lust.
And They, with the Daemons will be compelled to do everything in Their limited power
to complete the Great work (418) and build the structures and fortifications to
protect our Great and Beautiful New World...

By: Lacy Bryde

***Lacy not only speaks beautiful Art, but She also creates Art
as if the very Muses are guiding her hand.
Within her wonderful Art I can see the smile of Dionysus
and hear the Pipes of Pan.
Her beauty is just as powerful. I love you Lacy and thank
you for reminding me
that I'm a true descendant of Dionysus.*

Dionysus,

Hear me, we are drunk upon you; we will drink by our own will
and be lost and then found! Dionysus god of wine! Bless us on
this fruitful night! So we may drink and be happy!

Blessed be!

By: Luna Raven

The Sun Beneath The World

The almighty nocturnal flame, is the power that darkness has in the light to live with emotion in an emotionless world, is the desired fight pain offers itself to the weakness in me on an altar if fear, in return we follow his path with blood, sweat and tears, and as these liquids soak the grounds that our ancient ones built upon, realize the nourishment that it gave to the trees, breathes in, moves with ease, every step of the path releases oxygen from the blood that created the atmospheric breeze, the voice of the nocturnal flame is the infant's cry to return back into the darkness kidnapped by life, we tend to resent death, selfish, dark, empty and lonely, the purest part of mankind, the ultimate pleasure of your true self, given to you by the nocturnal flame, embrace the passion of the Dark, the heavy envelope that submerges your soul, let it rip you from who you think you are, travel the role of the mystery, the distance is not far, the guiding light is within, to stare within self is to stare into the flame, throw your fears into the fire, and release the pain.

By: Picasso

**Bro I'll never forget how WE appeased the gods during our Spring celebration.
While others cried, WE flew off the glory of the gods just bringing US together.

Dionysus

The wand with ivy twined about,
The cone of fire set high aloft,
Swift the maenads seek you out,
Through darkened forest, padding soft.

Tall trees and shafts of bluish light,
Merry they dance over leaf and cone.
Onward up the mountain's height,
Swift hooves now beat on grass and stone

Joy contagious. Pass the wine!
Blood of the grape. Blood of the land.
Drink from the cup, fruit of the vine,
Gift of the god to his merry band.

Spirit of earth, risen with the corn,
Head held high for the reaper's blade.
Solid flesh of the bull is torn,
Bursts like the grape and the earth's repaid.

Borne by dolphins through the deep.
Renewed. From the ocean life appears.
Nature quickens, wakes from sleep,
Summoned by trumpets, welcomed in tears.
A winnowing fan to cradle the king,

A boat on wheels his chariot made.
New hope and laughter, then suffering,
And flowers and fruit before him laid.

By: Liz Wesencraft

Dionysus,

Deep-hearted one who knows the souls of men and women,
whose hand is ever open, ever within reach.
Dionysus, god who runs in the dark, who sees with eyes shut tight,
who dances to the heart's strong beat, ever are you yourself,
ever constant, ever changing god of those who are trapped,
those who seek your truth in their own, those who seek vision beyond seeing,
those who seek wisdom beyond knowledge, those who seek the self, pure and sweet,
those who seek clarity beyond definition, who seek to embrace the uncertain,
to hold, but loosely, to what is true beyond trust.

By: Allison Roman

** My Ally Cat, the true embodiment of my goddess Diana. My Lady of the Hunt and Wild. I truly appreciate you sharing this beautiful prayer of our Lord. Surely He smiles upon your being as I smile upon your beauty.

I'll never forget all the chaotic Dionysian risk you took for me… Lol

Your gift in manipulating Art has transcended my world (get it?). I love you my Great Diana, my Roman goddess!!!

Dionysus Divine,

Ivy thick, twisted tight
A God half mortal
A God half Might
Bore my roots deep in dirt
Make my soul from fertile earth
My Blood shall flow as red as
Your wine
Faithful servant of
Dionysus Divine

By: Mercy

** Mercy I truly miss our beautiful Dark conversations we used to have. Where we discovered that we are born from a familiar place. I will meet you again in that familiar place where our shadows dance and our Daemons laugh. So until then, I'll bask in the Mercy of your nocturnal Light.

Dionysus,

Powerful and precious Dionysus PROTOGONOS,
first and last of Your kind- the Force of all titans and the Majesty of all gods.
Great Lord of both Men and Beasts, the one they call Dimorphon
who morphs between the two, who roars as the Promethean flame,
and rests silent as the grave in the fermented caves. Beast and beauty,
Bromios and Iakkhos, the Great God Who Comes, Come to us now,
One true Guardian, if only for one lesson and one alone: Teach us there is
no strife within the Heart that is Wild, and the wilderness that is the Heart.
That the sacred marriage of life and death, mud-born breath and soul-made eternity,
are both suckled strong by the mother's breast. That the holy desire
squeezed tight by Your glorious dragons, the self-forged Chronos and torch-bearing Ananke,
burns for one passion and one alone: To Remember the egg mistaken as dismembered.
Oh passion for life, plant this single truth in the heart again.
That the divine lives in the animal and Animal lives in the Divine.

...with love By: Dar Psyche Alexander

A Prayer,

Dionysus, make me drunk on the wine of life!
Open me up to every experience
so that when it is time to stand before the judges in the West
I will be able to say that I wasted not a second of life
and that I ended my days without a single regret.
Cause my spirit to overflow its bounds,
like the Nile spilling over its banks,
and may this inundation make the soil fertile
so that every type of crop and plant can take root in it.
Dionysus, nurture the seed that I plant and guide it until it reaches fruition.
Be just as gentle to me, Lord, as I undergo the journey into wholeness.
Show me the source of true being,
which survives every transformation,
even that of death,
so that I might see
just how small and powerless my fears are.

By: H. Jeremiah Lewis

**For over Ten years I've been actually reciting this Prayer to Dionysus.

When I first came across it, it touched me in ways that I knew made Dionysus proud.

I've learnt so much about Dionysus through the reading of H. Jeremiah Lewis' work.

I'll go as far as to say it's hard to say Dionysus' name without mentioning H. Jeremiah Lewis.

As a teen I devoured all his books and spent much time chanting to one day run into him at a Pagan Day Festival.

So if you ever read this H. Jeremiah Lewis, I'd like to say "Io Euoi Io Euoi Bios Dionusou!!!"

Soter

You are All I desire. Just embodying You changes everything in me, around me.

Longing for You makes me long to be free of anything that would pull my attention away.

I become One with Your many today. Thank You for promising to wear my flesh

as a representation of You. With You I am never alone. I adore Your enraptured Love, Kissos.

I admire Your beauty. With pleasure I draw wine from the grapes of Your wrath.

Teach me to make You the first place I run Mad to when I have cravings in my heart.

I don't want to waste time turning to other things that will never satisfy the need I have

for intimacy with You. My death awaits of You, Anthroporraistes...

Io Euoi !!!

** Soter is not just an epithet of Dionysus, He was Ptolemy I, or Ptolemy Soter, ruled Egypt from 323 to 285. He was born in 367 or 366 BCE in Makedonia, meaning he would have already been in his early forties when he became Pharaoh of Egypt. He ruled for thirty-eight years, so he was in his early eighties when he died. In 285 he gave up rule to his son, who had been co-regent for three years. He died three years after he retired.

'Amanda Aremisia Forrester' stated this about Ptolemy Soter:

The Neos Dionysus: The Ptolemies were descended from the god (Dionysus) and especially devoted to his cult. They embodied all of his qualities and several seemed to live entirely in his mythical shadow.

A Hindu might say that they were an avatar of Dionysus, the god made flesh on Earth. Many of the Ptolemies themselves claimed to be the New Dionysus. Soter, however, wasn't one of them. The Dionysian aspects of their kingship only became prominent with Philadelphos and it wasn't until the reign of Philopator that this term was even coined. That's not to say that Soter didn't worship the god or that Dionysian imagery played no part in his royal ideology – there is ample evidence in support of both points – but Soter was also, unquestionably, less of a Dionysian monarch than his descendants, especially since he tended more to favor the cults of Zeus and Herakles and modeled his rule after them. It may seem strange, then, to include him in this category, but when I've encountered the Neoi Dionysoi (or whatever the plural of the term would be) in ritual he's definitely been among them. Not as prominently as Philadelphos, Philopator, Auletes or Marcus Antonius, to be sure, but he nevertheless stands among them at their head, as is only fitting for the founder of the Dynasty. In terms of cultus the Neoi Dionysoi are a host of spirits resembling the god, sharing in his attributes, powers and personality as well as being distinct forms or masks through which he may manifest. Sometimes they appear all together as one being, like Dionysian nesting dolls stacked inside each other. Other times they are distinct, but form a troop or choir accompanying the god in his eternal revels. When Soter is among them he appears lighter, friendlier, more jubilant and, well, human – though it is his Dionysian qualities that are foremost. Lusty, laughing, dancing, drunk and joyous. This is my favorite side of him, but it's also the one I encounter least often. Of course it's not all fun and games – this is Dionysus we're talking about! – because there's also a solemnity and darkness beneath the mirth, and above all, a concern with fertility and especially the fertility of vegetative life through the process of death, decay and rebirth. Their revelry has a purpose – to awaken the dormant powers within the earth and stimulate growth and new green life once more.

Ancestral spirit: This is the form Soter takes when he is among the dead collectively. He is not one of the impotent and mindless shades of Haides – he's more like the powerful ancestral spirits of traditional African and Egyptian religion who dispense wisdom, luck and potency when appeased, but send illness, death and calamity when ignored. This form is very different from the others I've encountered. It's much less personal, to the point where it can be difficult to distinguish him from the other spirits. He's more a force or power than anything, driven by hunger and craving attention. But not personal attention, since there's little that's personal left to him. It's blood and dance and offerings of food and alcohol and attention for all the dead that he desires, and he is just one among many. A host of souls continuing to influence this world from beyond the grave. The dead are dark and strange and hungry but they show great kindness to those who feed them. They are especially effective in healing illness, sending prophetic dreams and increasing one's luck.

Ptolemy Soter himself: This is probably the form that I've encountered least often, but in some ways it's left the greatest impression on me. This is just Ptolemy the son of Lagos. Not the king, not the god, not the living image of Dionysus or the great ancestral spirit – but the man. A man born in the hinterlands of Greece many centuries ago, who spent most of his life on the battlefield, who loved his wives and mistresses, who wanted only the best for his children and looked back with pride on the incredible things he'd done and seen over his eighty-plus years. He was a man of keen intellect, though not an intellectual by any stretch of the imagination. He was interested in figuring out how things worked – but only if that knowledge had a practical application. Others could spend time with their heads in the clouds – he was too busy keeping his men alive or governing a country. He was a stern patriarch, a man of honesty, integrity and uncompromising moral convictions. A hard man, disciplined and frugal. He didn't shun wealth, but he believed that it should be used properly, never allowing it to corrupt one's character or be pursued as an end unto itself. He demanded much of those around him – especially his children – but demanded even more of himself. He was interested in other cultures, especially when it came to their religious beliefs, but in the end he was a deeply conservative soul who believed in the inherent superiority of his people and their traditions. He was like your grandfather. Someone who came through the Great Depression, fought in WWII and Korea and had the scars and stories to show for it. Hard, but not cruel; kind, but not doting. Set in his ways, a little crabby, but with a ready smile and a booming, infectious laugh. Full of solid practical advice – whether asked for or not – and more than a little nostalgic, frequently going on about how much better things were back in his day, yet grudgingly impressed by the progress we've made in certain areas. Over all, a wise and good man you'd do well to listen to.

The Charge Of Dionysus

"Io Euoi, Io Euoi, Bios Dionusou. Behold and take heed to the ecstatic words of the Horned god, who is the Divine child of the Dark fertile Earth, Semele, our Lady. He who is the Guardian of All things Erotic, Wild, Free and of Blessed Deliverance, the keeper of the Gates of sensuality, who gives us blissful enthusiasm for life, who guides us all to drink from His nectar witch is the elixir of the gods."

"I am the Lord of the erotic dance of life, death and rebirth, the drunken reaper, the Vine and the essence of Nature. All things wild and free are of Me, for I am of the Goddess—Opposite, however never opposing. I am both the raw flesh of the sacrificial animal and the Wine which is drunk in My honor. I am the grapes that ripen and I am the reaper of those grapes in the Fall, and I am reborn in life as the Divine child that springs forth anew from the fields of My Mother. I am the Frenzy of the pleasurable dance between life and death. I am the Prince of the underworld, where no living being may venture, and I am also the Prince of Rebirth and make of death a life. My domain is extended to all of Nature and its life-giving and seminal moisture, the sap rising in a tree, the blood pounding in the veins, the liquid fire of the grape, all the Mysterious and uncontrollable tides that flow and ebb in Nature. I bring blessed ecstasy and enraptured love to those who tolerate the full range from death to life and from pain to ecstasy, who recognize and appreciate the place of pain and death, carnal lust and psychedelic spiritual life. The true Body of Me comes from the pleasurable hearts and desires of my people and not from any book of Law. I lead all that die into the frenzied dance that returns us all to life. I am the Priest of the Great Goddess Cybele and the herald of all that comes from Her. I am the fiery desire within all hearts, the yearning of pleasure, the essence of getting lost in the moment of a sexual exchange. I who stand in the Darkness of Night am He whom you called Death.

"I am the Son of Her we adore and cherish. Heed My call, beloved ones of desire, come unto Me and learn the secrets of Ecstasy and Holy Madness, Wildness and of the most Blessed Deliverance, of Death and Peace. I am He who leads you to your rawest Nature. Spontaneous sensuality and Wine, Free Love and Disruptive Passion. These are Mine and gifts to you to cherish. Call unto Me in the forest wild and amongst the mist of Nature and seek Me in the Darkness bright. I who have been called Dionysus, Bacchus, Zagreus, Karneios and Lacchus to you in your search will give you freedom from conventional mores and taboos, so to allow a natural ecstatic expression of the inner self in a ritualized process. In My honor, allow this process to involve the nectar of Me(Wine), wild music, theater, frenzied movements of dance, orgies that will overcome your ordinary inhibitions. For My ecstatic experiences will provide you with a sense of a spiritual Oneness that underlie reality, of being part of Me, Nature and part of humanity. Drink of Me and free oneself from material cares and allow it to be a mystical pleasure that frees oneself momentarily from your inhibitions, attachments and ties. Lose yourself within My Nature and be transcendent to another subjectively felt ecstatic realm.

I am He who rescues and restores women back to their natural Divine state. For in the days of old it was women who kept My ways alive. And for that they shall be honored, cherished and respected at all times. And before My Mother evolved them into women, they were My Panthers (sacred animal), so whenever ye see a Panther let that be a reminder that women are just as equally a part of Me as men are. Now come dance and sing, come live and smile, love and be loved, please and be pleased, desire and be desired-this is My worship. However, my beloved ones, there is no one right way to celebrate Me, All have value and All can potentially inspire some new methods of pleasure and blessed deliverance. Nor do I promise to show you the One true path for the simple reason that the only true path is the One you forge yourself within the essence of Me. With swift Night wings, it is I who lay you at Our Mother's feet to be reborn. You who think to pleasure Me, know that I am the untamed Wildwood, the fury of Nature and Passion in your flesh. Seek Me with pleasure and ecstasy, but seek me best with enraptured love and beautiful courage. Hear My call on long Dark Winter Nights and We shall stand together drunken in passion guarding Her Earth as She sleeps.

Io Euoi, Io Euoi, Bios Dionusou!!!!

**When I speak on 'disruptive passion' in this Charge, I'm speaking on the role of Dionysus when He disrupts people's lives, taking them out of their normal lives, so to get them to revel in Nature, pleasure, music and dance. So, don't misinterpret 'disruptive passion' with violent passion. This Charge was inspired by many Charges. This Charge is only a means of inspiration to those connected to Dionysus...

By: John 'Karneios' Auletta

Epithets Of Dionysus

(His Many Masks)

Epithets: Agrios (The Wild One), Aigobolos (The Goatslayer), Aktaios (He of the Seacoast), Anax Bakcheios (Bacchic Lord), Anax Agreus (Lord Hunter), Antheus (The Blossoming), Anthroporraistes (The Render of Humans), Areion (War-like), Arretos (The Ineffable), Arsenothelys (the Man-Womanly), Auxites (The Grower), Axios Tauros (The Worthy Bull), Bakcheios (The Bacchic One), Bakchos (Raving), Bassareus (The Fox-God), Botryophoros (Bearer of Clusters of Grapes), Boukeros (The Bull-horned One), Bromios (He Who Roars), Bythios (The Deep), Charidotes (The Giver of Grace), Choreutes (The Dancer), Choroplekes (The Danceweaving One), Chthonios (He of the Underworld), Dendrites (The Tree God), Dikerotes (The Two-horned One), Dimeter (He of Two Mothers), Dimorphos (The Two-Formed One), Dissotokos (Doubly Born), Dithyrambos (Hymned by the Dithyramb), Eiraphiotes (The In-Sewn One), Ekstatophoros (The Bringer of Ecstasy), Eleuthereus (The Emancipator), Enorches (the Betesticled), Eriphos (Young Kid), Eribromios (The Loud Roarer), Euanthes

(The Fair Blossoming One), Euaster (He Who Shouts Eua), Eubouleus (The Good Counselor), Euios (The Reveler), Gethosynos (The Joyful), Gigantophonos (Giant-Slayer), Gynnis (Womanish), Hagnos (The Pure, Holy One), Iakchos (The Cryer at Eleusis), Iatros (The Healer), Karneios (Horned Sun), Kissobryos (The Ivy-Wrapped One), Kissokomes (The Ivy-Crowned One), Kissos (Ivy), Korymbophoros (The Cluster-laden), Kryphios (The Hidden One), Lampter (Light-bringer), Lenaios (He of the Wine-press), Liknites (He of the Winnowing Fan Cradle), Limnaios (He of the Marsh), Lyaios (Bringer of Freedom), Lyseus (Liberator), Mainomenos (The Maddened One), Makar (Blessed One), Manikos (The Manic One), Mantis (The Diviner), Meilichios (The Gentle One), Melanaigis (He of the Black Goatskin), Morychos (The Dark One), Nebrodes (The Fawn-form One), Nyktelios (He of the Night), Nyktipolos (The Night-Stalker), Nysios (He of Nysa), Oiketor (The Indweller), Omadios (He of the Raw Feast), Palaios (The Ancient One), Perikionios (He Who is Entwined Around the Pillars), Petempamenti (He who is in the Underworld), Phanes (The Illuminator), Polygethes (Bringer of Many Joys), Polymorphos (He of the Many Forms), Polyonomos (The Many-Named One), Protogonos (The Firstborn), Skeptouchos (Scepter-Bearer), Soter (Savior), Sykites (He of the Fig-Tree), Taurokeros Theos (Bull-horned God), Taurophagos (Devourer of the Bull), Tauropon (The Bull-faced One), Teletarches (Lord of Initiation), Thyonidas (Son of Thyone), Thyrsophoros (The Thyrsos-Bearer),

Trieterikos (The Biennial One), Trigonos (The Thrice born), Zagreus (Great Hunter), Zatheos (The Very Holy), Zoophoros (Life Bringer)

Equated With: Osiris, Serapis, Apis, Set, Adonis, Antinous, Yahweh, Priapus, Ba¡⁻al, Siva, Katagarma, Ptolemy IV, Ptolemy XII, Marcus Antonius, Attalos.

Associations: thyrsos, mask, nebrix, kantharos, phallos, panther, goat, snake, bull, fox, musk, civet, frankincense, storax, ivy, grapes, pine, fig, wine, honey, Indian hemp, orchis root, thistle, all wild and domestic trees, black diamond.

KNOWN FACTS ABOUT DIONYSUS

(Just To Name A Few)

Dionysus was primarily known as the God of the Vine.

He was also referred to as Bacchus.

Dionysus and DEMETER, the Goddess of the Corn, were the supreme deities of the Earth.

Unlike the immortal gods, who were often hostile toward human beings, Dionysus and Demeter were benevolent toward mankind.

Dionysus was the younger of the two, and little is known about how he came to take his place beside Demeter to be worshipped.

Dionysus and Demeter were worshipped at Eleusis, a little town near Athens.

Dionysus was a happy god during the harvest, but during the winter he languished along with the rest of the Earth.

Dionysus was the last god to enter Olympus.

Dionysus was the son of Zeus and the Theban princess Semele. He was the only god who had a mortal parent.

He was born in Thebes.

He was born of fire and nursed by rain. His birth corresponds to the development of grapes: heat ripens the fruit and water keeps it alive.

Upon reaching adulthood, Dionysus wandered the Earth, teaching men the culture of the vine.

Many festivals were held in honor of Dionysus: the Lesser or Rural Dionysia, the Greater or City Dionysia, the Anthesteria, and the Lenaea.

Dionysus was variously represented in art as a full-grown bearded man, as a beast, and as a slight youth.

Dionysus was insulted by Lycurgus, one of the kings in Thrace. Dionysus initially retreated and took refuge in the sea, but later he imprisoned Lycurgus for opposing his worship.

Performances of tragedy and comedy were a part of the festivals thrown in his honor.

Dionysus was also honored in lyric poetry How I'm honoring Him now).

Dionysus was once captured by pirates, because he looked like the son of a king. They kidnapped him, envisioning the ransom his parents would pay upon his return. Aboard the ship, the pirates were unable to confine him. The ropes fell apart when they touched Dionysus.

Dionysus rescued the princess of Crete, Ariadne, and subsequently fell in love with her. Upon her death, Dionysus placed the crown he had given her among the stars.

Though Dionysus was mostly a kind and generous deity, he could be cruel when necessary. Pentheus, a king of Thebes, tried to stop the frenzied worship of Dionysus. He attempted to imprison the God of Wine, while hurling insults and accusations at him. Dionysus explained his own eminence calmly, but Pentheus was unreceptive. Dionysus caused the Theban women to go mad so that they thought Pentheus a wild beast. They tore Pentheus limb from limb.

A Dionysian Afterthought

(My Underworld Journey)

"Our ancient ancestors created myths to explain reality in their own unique way, making creation conscious of itself."

Being Dionysian Pagan alone is to be deeply rooted to the Earth, connected to Her in ways others can't understand. Feeling that fire within the core of Earth pull at your very wild heart, so just imagine being a Pagan with that type of connection cut off from the Earth? Wild right? That's like a Witch without a Moon. This is how it felt when I first got incarcerated. Oh, you didn't know? I'm a Dionysian Pagan who just happens to be incarcerated. And when I first got locked up, I cursed every trickster god known to man for putting me in such a place. Shit, I cursed myself for putting me in such a situation. Then one day on the prison yard as I gazed at the trees and birds, it hit me. As a Dionysian Pagan we see wisdom and sacredness in all things. So I began to look deeper into my situation. I looked deeper into myself and realized that I'm not the only one who has took similar journeys like this one. Suddenly my incarceration became my journey into the underworld, a path inward. A journey that many goddesses, gods and heroes of the old days made. The goddess Inanna descended to the underworld so to better understand Her darker self (which is only Her sister Eriskegal). In this way She learns what She needs to know of Her other half which now makes Her whole.

Dionysus descended to the underworld to both save His wife and mother, restoring Them back to Their Divine state and while at the same time becoming physical and spiritual food Himself for His people. My incarceration (twenty-three-hour lockdown) forced me to take the inward journey into my underworld where I found the feminine aspect of myself I've been ignoring for a while. Once I embraced my inner feminine nature I became whole, which in the process restored my inner feminine self, just as Dionysus did. See myths reveal the structure of reality. Myths provide information about ourselves as a culture and as species. So my inner journey began to mirror those of the ancients, which gives me hope in such a place. My inward path became the 'Night Journey Of The Soul' which speaks to the need of individuals to descend into the self, so to face the aspects that have been ignored. In ancient myths when Perseus faces Medusa and decapitates Her and when Theseus defeats the Minotaur, their actions are in the psychological sense, metaphors, for facing my own inner dark aspects of self that I have ignored or denied. The fact that ancient heroes are helped by the gods in some of their descended journeys symbolize the 'Divine' potential within myself, to face and embrace what has been denied or ignored.

Contrary to popular perception, the inner shadow (dark self) may contain desirable as well as undesirable things. It may hold power and gifts—things we have kept at bay to make ourselves more acceptable to this twisted judgmental society.

So the mythical goddess, gods and heroes' descent into the underworld became my descent into the dark world of prison, of my inner self—so to find a way to my wholeness. I gave my prison experience a sacred conscious meaning in my own unique way which is inspired by the myths of our gods. The mythical goddess, gods and heroes return (rebirth from the underworld), is my achievement to my wholeness and wisdom. Being rebirth as 'Karneios' The rebirth or return from the underworld is always with something gained or learned

The goddess Inanna returns from the underworld with a fuller knowledge of the whole world She rules, rather than just the positive side of Nature. The gods Dionysus and Osiris return from the underworld as sources of material and spiritual food for Their people. Within this descent, I have learned much which caused me to see that even though I'm physically disconnected from Earth, I'm not fully disconnected from the goddess and Her wisdom, Dionysus and His pleasures. They've both shown me that in my situation, meditation and symbolic actions are also expressions of Them.

Some people may belittle my concept of sacred meditation being an expression of Them both, but it should be understood that I'm acting in part of both Her and Dionysus principal that everything is connected and They are also ' within as well as without '.

What happens in the privacy of my mental state, is connected to every other part of this interconnected Universe (The Great Goddess). A change in understanding or motivation is already a change in the web of all things. Since this web and Universe is full of life, the change is one of relationship. So what begins as 'thinking nice things—a good imagination' begins to affect world views and effect change in lifestyle. This type of unique Dionysian Pagan perception keeps my hope alive within this wild place. It works for me!!

~~*~*

I would like to close out by saying, my quotes, adages, poetry and jewels are forms of inspiration. Majority of the quotes are originally mine and others were adopted, yet I added my own Dionysian Pagan twist to it. That's nothing new though, throughout history, wise ones have adopted other people's quotes yet while putting their own twist to them. This is how famous quotes made their way down to us, through the process of change and unique repolishing. For example: A Dutch proverb says, "He who has a head of butter must not come near the oven." That was adopted and twisted in a way, to say, "If you can't stand the heat keep out of the kitchen." It's like resetting a worn out gem (old quote) in a new setting and suddenly sparkling something new. And my aim was to adopt some old quotes (worn out) and re-sparkle them anew with a Dionysian Pagan twist. Beautiful quotes inspire the world. Did Gandhi's quotes of wisdom (non-violent protest) not help inspire Martin L. King? My goal is to give the next generation of Dionysian Pagans some beautiful quotes, prayers, and adages to be inspired by. When you go through a crisis, your instincts are to turn to your roots. And we are now the roots of our future Pagans in generations to come. So, within any moment of crisis that may come their way, I want the root of my quotes, adages and poetry to inspire them to overcome their crisis. I want to pass down wisdom of Dionysus and the gods through the unique creation of my quotes. As Pagans we know how powerful words can be. Look at how 'The Charge of The Goddess' has shaped our Pagan community.

Due to my incarcerated situation, I'm doing the best I can to give back to my Pagan community. I chant, "Io Euoi," that y'all are proud of me. I'm just expressing the gift that Dionysus bestowed upon me. The gift to reach out with ecstatic words which calls women out of their normal lives, so to get them to revel within the bliss of Nature—restoring them back to their Divine state. However, not only women, but also restoring the feminine aspect (inner goddess) within men.

On another note, I would love to hear your comments and thoughts on this book. Please connect me via email: sunofdionysus@gmail.com

Or my IG:@sunofdionysus. Thanks for your time.

Io Euoi Io Euoi Bios Dionusou !!!!!

About The Author

John Phillip Auletta (1985 –),

John Phillip Auletta also known as 'Karneios' by Dionysus and the gods. A distinguished Dionysian Pagan and Initiate of The Way Of The Satyr. A modern Patron of the Technitai Dionusou and was one of the original founders of 'ATD' (Auric of Transcendent Divinity) which is now a small community of eclectic Witches, Wiccans and Dionysian Pagans whose Transcendence is based on Dance, Music, Psychedelic Ritual and ecstatic sex. Also a Co-Founding member of 'Heretic Witchcraft'—that started out as a Cyber E-Net Coven online. His most widely-known works include 'Loyalty Is Everything' (an Amazon E-Book which was a fiction memoir based on some actual events of his youthful life. His aim in writing it was to teach the youth of the dangerous manipulation and violence within gangs). Also has his Pagan Wisdom featured within many foundations, such as: Pen America, Prisons Foundation and The American Prison Archive. All in all, he's a very active and loving Dionysian Pagan, despite his incarceration...

Printed in Great Britain
by Amazon